ZANZIBAR PLATES

Maastricht and Other Ceramics on the East African Coast

ALSO BY VILLOO NOWROJEE

A Select Bibliography of Asian African Writing

ALSO BY PHEROZE NOWROJEE

Pio Gama Pinto: Patriot for Social Justice

A Vote for Kenya: The Elections and the Constitution

A Kenyan Journey

Conserving the Intangible

Dukawalla and Other Stories

ZANZIBAR PLATES

Maastricht and Other Ceramics
on the East African Coast

Villoo Nowrojee
Pheroze Nowrojee

MANQA
books

NAIROBI

Published by Manqa Books
www.manqa.net

Editing by Edward Miller
Cover and book design by Edward Miller
All photos and images copyright © Villoo Nowrojee unless otherwise indicated
All photos and images by Edward Miller unless otherwise indicated
Text set in Garamond Premier Pro

First Edition
10 9 8 7 6 5

This book is dedicated to

SADIQ GHALIA

and

CHRIS and TERESA ORME-SMITH

INTRODUCTION

THEY SPEAK TO us of warm welcomes and traditional hospitality, of large offerings of richly flavoured rice, of meat cooked in coconut milk, of sweets as generous in quantity as the meals they followed.

Bright purple flowers and leaves in a deep green rim a serving dish. Blue buds and grey stalks decorate a big plate. Stylized lotuses in red, black, and green circle a bowl. The fine mosaic of fired clay, aged brown surfaces, and the patina of use all add to making each item an extremely desirable collectible.

These attractive objects have been in our region since the second half of the 19th century. Searches in the antique shops of Zanzibar, Mombasa, Dar es Salaam, and Nairobi will be repaid by colourful plates and bowls, and, less often, cups and saucers. They are not works of fine art, and do not pretend to the refinement and beauty of Chinese porcelain. But they are objects that give enormous pleasure, happily rekindling expectations of orange-coloured halwa with shelled almonds for tea and old-time hospitality for company at many a dining table today.

Though casually called 'Zanzibar plates', they are neither plates nor made in Zanzibar. Most are really dishes. And they were made principally in Holland, England, Germany, and France, with lesser contributions from other countries, including Belgium and Japan.

They have been in use and can still be found today in many countries of the Indian Ocean, from Madagascar, Yemen, and India to Indonesia. Although they were widely found all over the Swahili coast, and originally had been imported into East Africa directly by all the cities, notably Lamu, 'Zanzibar's policy of centralizing all imports and exports through her own warehouses left Lamu [and other ports] far behind. The inadequacy of Lamu's port facilities for the steamship age...were contributory causes to [the] decline [of her traditional maritime trade].'[1]

1 James de Vere Allen, *Lamu Town: A Guide* (Lamu, National Museums of Kenya, 1977), 9.

Thus in the region of the East African coast, the principal place of importation, and the principal local source, became Zanzibar. As a result, they have often been referred to as 'Zanzibar plates',[2] and the term remains a convenient alternative to clumsy and long definitions of greater accuracy.

2 See for example Judith Aldrick, 'The Painted Plates of Zanzibar' (1997), 29, in *Kenya Past and Present*, 26. In much the same way, and for the same reasons, Chinese blue-and-white ceramics were in the last century in East Africa 'often, quite wrongly, known as "Lamu ware", because it was once thought that Lamu was the main centre of import' (G. S. P. Freeman-Grenville, 'Chinese Porcelain in Tanganyika', in *Tanganyika Notes and Records* No. 41, December 1955, 64).

CERAMICS IN EAST AFRICA

PORCELAIN AND other ceramics have been an East African import for many centuries. The earliest of such imports were not these plates. The early imports were from Persia[1] and then from China, and both of these preceded Zanzibar plates by hundreds of years. However, to understand the uses to which the later Maastricht and other ceramics were put in East Africa, it is necessary to understand the uses to which the earlier ware from Persia and China had been put in the region.

PERSIAN WARE

Glazed ware from Persia was in use on the East African coast consequent upon the long-established Indian Ocean trade. Sassanian-Islamic ware has been found in tenth century CE and subsequent levels, among other places at Kilwa.[2] Other glazed ware (16th century CE) from Persia has also been recovered at Gedi.[3] Their valued and decorative use is dealt with below.

These are the earliest ceramics on the East African coast, and they have the added importance and value of being instruments for the dating of the archaeological remains. As noted by James Kirkman in assessing certain monuments in Pemba, 'the date of the beginning of the settlement depends on the dating of the Islamic yellow *sgraffiato* found below the foundation of Tomb A.'[4]

This is true of ceramics as a whole. For 'East African history is poorly documented and the paucity of written records makes coinage almost the only link, with porcelain, between archaeology and its recorded history'.[5]

CHINESE WARE

Chinese porcelain and ceramics were a regular part of the trade between China and India. From there they became an early part of the trade between India and the East African coast, so that, while

1 For which see Charles K. Wilkinson, *Iranian Ceramics* (New York, Asia House Gallery Publications, 1963).

2 Neville Chittick, 'Notes on Kilwa', *Tanganyika Notes and Records* No. 53 (October 1959), 179; Karen Moon, *Kilwa Kisiwani: Ancient Port City of the East African Coast* (Dar es Salaam, Government of Tanzania, 2005).
3 James Kirkman, 'Fort Jesus Museum Collection', *Kenya Past and Present* Vol. 1 No. 2 (April 1972), 4.

4 James Kirkman, 'Excavations at Ras Mkumbuu on the Island of Pemba' in *Tanganyika Notes and Records* No. 53 (October 1959), 161, at 170.
5 Dr. G. S. P. Freeman-Grenville, 'Some Problems of East African Coinage: From Early Times to 1890', *Tanganyika Notes and Records* No. 53 (October 1959), 250.

utilitarian pottery had arrived earlier, by the 14th century CE fine Chinese porcelain items were prized items on the East African coast.

This was as much for their intrinsic beauty as because of the absence of glazed pottery at the coast. Local pottery was not glazed. Such imported pottery, however, was an expensive luxury, at once decorative and durable. Only the most affluent households could possess wares from China. In time, their presence, worth, and beauty came to reflect more than just evidence of good taste at the table. Plates began to be displayed in the house as wall decorations and objects of status. Well-to-do houses had plates and bowls placed in niches around certain rooms. Some came to be embedded in the walls.[6]

In *Al-Inkishafi*, the famous poem written around 1820 in Pate, while mourning its lost greatness, the poet Sayyid Abdalla bin Ali bin Nasir, in enumerating aspects of Pate's former prosperity, says the following:

38 Wapambiye sini ya kuteuwa,
na kula kikombe kinakishiwa;
Kati watiziye kuzi za kowa,
katika mapambo yanawiriye.
They decorated with choicest porcelain,
And every cup embellished;
They placed crystal pitchers in the centre,
To glitter there amidst the things of beauty.[7]

On this stanza, James de Vere Allen in his translation of the poem writes: 'At the beginning of the present [20th] century many bowls were still embedded in private houses (although the vast majority have since been either looted or broken in attempts by curio-hunters to prise them out). A great number of others were either used or displayed in wealthy houses, and evidently in the Swahili world, as in several other Indian Ocean societies, social prestige was almost invariably registered by the amount of imported pottery one was able to display. So close is the correlation between prosperity and imported pottery that archaeologists can gauge with reasonable accuracy the wealth of any given site on the East African coast by the ratio of imported to local ware. In Pate

6 Judith Aldrick, 'The Painted Plates of Zanzibar' (1997), *29 Kenya Past and Present,* 26.
7 Sayyid Abdalla bin Ali bin Nasir, *Al-Inkishafi: Catechism of a Soul*, transl. James de Vere Allen (Nairobi, EA Literature Bureau, 1977).

town the ratio is very high for the late seventeenth and eighteenth centuries. Glass is also found, but it is less easily dated. Some engraved goblets and bowls which may well date from this period have also survived and are in the Lamu Museum collection.'[8]

*

In respect of the removed and damaged porcelain on tombs at Kilwa, Chittick remarked, 'It seems that such trophy-hunting both here and elsewhere is chiefly to be ascribed to visitors in the last century. It is clear from the records of the German administration that many of these acts of vandalism had already occurred before 1904.'[9]

Twenty years earlier Robinson had noted, 'These Shirazi sites are now avoided by natives who have not

scrupled to remove the bowls for sale to travelers until the supply has been exhausted... Some of the bowls which have been removed are now in London and other museums where they are exhibited as samples of Chinese art.'[10]

James de Vere Allen noted, 'Regrettably, a very large number of such pieces were removed by Nineteenth Century European explorers or early Twentieth Century European administrators, who did not hesitate in some cases to destroy the building to do so. The majority that remain have been removed since, generally so inexpertly that they are broken in the process, by local people who seek to sell them to tourists for trifling sums. Where they remain, however, even fragmentarily, they are of great assistance in dating buildings. Plates continued to be set into

8 Ibid.
9 Neville Chittick, 'Notes on Kilwa' in *Tanganyika Notes and Records* No. 53 (1959), 179.

10 Arthur E. Robinson, 'Notes on Saucer and Bowl Decorations on Houses, Mosques and Temples' in *Tanganyika Notes and Records* No. 10 (December 1940), 79, 85.

mosque walls as late as the end of the Nineteenth Century.'[11]

UTILITARIAN CHINESE WARE

Commenting on this use of china in these households, James de Vere Allen in another text repeats his earlier-mentioned point: 'It was customary in wealthy Swahili homes (as in those of so many other Indian Ocean societies) to register one's wealth and taste by a display of fine imported glazed pottery. Such a hard and fast rule is this that, where a settlement was wealthy, one can be absolutely sure that a great number of fragments will remain in its ruins, and where there are no such fragments for a period covering, say, two centuries, one can be equally sure that during those

centuries the settlement was in economic decline.'[12]

But surviving objects and shards, found over the north coast of Kenya, testify that the imports from China were not all or always of fine Chinaware. Less fine, more utilitarian objects also reached the East African coast and were in use there from a much earlier period. The Orme-Smith Collection provides examples of these large pots, glazed and unglazed, some exhibited now in the Gedi and Malindi Museums.

Chris Orme-Smith writes: 'Coarser, more utilitarian pottery from China was also in use on the East African Coast during this period. The Orme-Smith Collection has examples of these, collected mainly from Lamu, Malindi,

Kipini and Takaungu. Large quantities of this pottery was over the centuries imported up and down the East African Coast and was affordable to all.

'Often, and wrongly, referred to as "Lamu China", the pottery has as little to do with Lamu as the much later appearance of the Zanzibar Plates have with Zanzibar! It seems likely that the early visitors from Europe to Lamu were impressed by the abundance of Chinese pottery in use, which led to this misconception that the pottery was actually produced there.

'Whilst it is difficult these days to find intact items of pottery, every coastal settlement, however humble, has its midden which often yields a rich varied assortment of shards, which could date from the 9th Century CE to the

11 James de Vere Allen, *Lamu* (Nairobi, Kenya Museum Society, 1972), 22–23.

12 Ibid. 23.

present day. Such a settlement is the little visited fishing village of Takaungu situated on a high promontory overlooking a creek some distance from the open sea and south of Kilifi.

'For centuries, the villagers have been throwing their refuse over the cliffs into the mangrove swamp below, and they still do so today. Shards found on a beach are inevitably smoothed and seaworn, whilst those in the turgid muddy waters of the mangrove swamp are in pristine condition, excavated on a daily basis by the large crabs common to the area.

'Most of the items I have recovered from this area are Chinese pottery dating from the late 15th Century CE to the late 19th, several 15th Century glass flasks (necks and bases) from Damascus, 11th Century green Islamic

glazed ware, 17th Century glazed Chinese scent bottles, not to mention numerous beads from China, India and the Middle East, some of which had not previously been recorded anywhere on the East African Coast.'[13]

James Kirkman draws the same conclusion. 'The appearance of Chinese porcelain from as early as the ninth century, considering the distance, is one of the surprises of East African archaeology. It could not have been very expensive because it is found in such quantity, yet the business was profitable or it would not have been undertaken.'[14]

This also reminds us that Indian Ocean trade patterns are of extremely long standing, and that Chinese porcelain was in use in East Africa centuries before Europe came to know of it.[15]

ON PILLAR TOMBS AND MOSQUES

In funerary architecture, Chinese plates and bowls were also embedded in tomb walls and tomb pillars and mosques. Famous, and typical, examples of these may be seen in the Mambrui ruins, the Gedi (Gede) ruins, both on the Kenyan north coast, and at Kunduchi near Dar es Salaam.[16]

The Chinese plate on

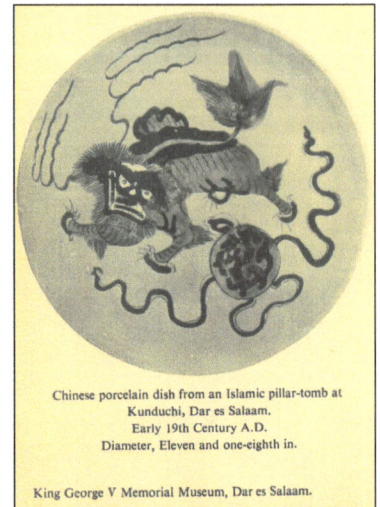

Chinese porcelain dish from an Islamic pillar-tomb at Kunduchi, Dar es Salaam.
Early 19th Century A.D.
Diameter, Eleven and one-eighth in.

King George V Memorial Museum, Dar es Salaam.

Elchi Nowrojee Collection

Postcard of a Chinese porcelain dish from the early 19th century found on an Islamic pillar tomb in Kunduchi, Dar es Salaam.

the Kunduchi pillar tomb is illustrated on a postcard circa 1948, from the (then) King George V Memorial Museum, (now the National Museum of Tanzania) in Dar es Salaam, titled 'Chinese porcelain dish from an Islamic pillar-tomb at Kunduchi, Dar es Salaam' (see illustration).

The pillar tomb at the ruins at Mambrui north of Malindi still retains its Chinese porcelain dishes in situ (see illustrations).

13 Personal communication, August 2006.
14 James Kirkman, 'Fort Jesus Museum Collection', *Kenya Past and Present*, Vol. 1, No. 2 (April 1972), 4. For the early dating see also Hamo Sassoon, 'The Coastal Town of Jumba La Mtwana', 12, *Kenya Past and Present* 2 (1980), 13: 'The earliest examples on the Kenya Coast have been found at Manda in the Lamu region and are dated in the ninth century.' See also H. Neville Chittick, 'Unguja Ukuu: The Earliest Imported Pottery and One Abbasid Dinar', *Azania* I (1966), 161.

15 R. J. Charleston (ed.), *English Porcelain 1745–1850* (London, Ernest Benn/University of Toronto, 1965), 17.
16 See Plate 21 of the tomb with inset Chinese bowls (and inscribed with the date 1162 AH–1748-49 CE) illustrating Neville Chittick, 'Relics of the Past in the Region of Dar-es-Salaam', in Dar-es-Salaam City, Port and Region' *Tanganyika Notes and Records* No. 71 (1970), 65; Hamo Sassoon, *Kunduchi: A Guide to the Ruins at Kunduchi* (Dar es Salaam, Ministry of Community Development and National Culture, 1966), 2. See also Richard Wilding, 'The Ceramics of the Lamu Archipelago' (1977), PhD thesis, University of Nairobi, 557ee et and Plates 653–656.

Left: The pillar tomb at Gedi.
Above: The *mihrab* at Gedi, showing the indentations where the plates had been fixed.
Below, left and right: Chinese porcelain dishes in the pillar tomb at Mambrui.

The Gedi ruins have no plates and bowls in situ, the remnants being displayed in the museum at Gedi and in Fort Jesus, but the very visible indentations around the *mihrabs* in the mosques and on the pillar tombs show clearly where these bowls had been placed and how many of these ornamentations there were originally. In 1949, in the first publication on Gedi for public use at the site, J. S. Kirkman wrote, '...the Mihrab was originally decorated with porcelain bowls, but these have all gone. On the east side of the mosque there is the usual layout of mosque precincts: well, conduit, cistern and lavatory, the whole enclosed by a boundary wall... Inside the cistern is a celadon bowl; hitherto, the only bowl at Gedi found in position.'[17]

This beautiful bowl can be seen among the exhibits in the Small Museum, Gedi.

17 *Gedi National Park: Plan and Explanatory Notes* (Nairobi, Government Printer, Kenya National Parks Trustees, Government Printer, March 1949).

Pillar tombs in Pemba were also recorded with bowls still in place. Pearce noted them[18] on his first visit, but by the time he visited them again the bowls had been removed from the pillars. Later, Kirkman documented that Pemba's Pillar Tomb D 'is square with three bowl cavities and it was capped with a square finial which may once have supported a jar...The top of Pillar Tomb C is broken and may once have held a porcelain bowl.'[19] The circa 1978 photographic record by Esmond Bradley Martin also confirms the original presence of bowls on the 15th century CE pillar tombs at Ras Mkumbu in Pemba.[20]

Prior to the installation of china and other plates, it was one practice, if the *mihrabs* were embellished at all, for the *mihrabs* to be inscribed with calligraphic inscriptions from the Holy Quran. One such example survives at Dimbani village next to Kizimkazi in the south of Zanzibar island, "the site of a Shirazi [Persian] mosque dating from the early 12th century and considered to be one of the oldest Islamic buildings on the East African coast, although much of what [is seen] today is restorations carried out in the 1770s. The Quran verses inscribed in the *mihrab* date to 1107 and are among the oldest known examples of Swahili writing.'[21]

Chittick has noted that previously the Swahili had used carved round coral blocks as decorations on walls and mosques, in *mihrabs*, and on graves and tombs. Fine examples of these coral blocks from Jumba la Mtwana,[22] Kongo Mosque, and Mnarani can be seen at the museum at Gedi.

Another may be seen in the Lamu Museum. Chittick posited that the practice of embedding imported plates in preference to the carved blocks led to the decline of the Swahili coral stone carving tradition.

Hamo Sassoon refers to pillar tombs as 'a peculiarity of the East African Coast'. Wilding considers that the ceramic insets argue in all cases for a post–14th century date, and reminds us that pillar tombs are not found earlier than the 13th century and that 'at no time did such tombs represent more than a small proportion of interments.'[23] Pillar tombs were built in the 15th century CE (at Kaole near Bagamoyo),[24] as in the

18 Major Francis Barrow Pearce, *Zanzibar: The Island Metropolis of Eastern Africa* (London, 1920).
19 James Kirkman, 'Excavations at Ras Mkumbuu on the Island of Pemba', *Tanganyika Notes and Records* No. 53 (October 1959), 161, 168.
20 Esmond Bradley Martin, *Zanzibar, Tradition and Revolution* (London, Hamish Hamilton, 1998), 118–119.

21 Mary Fitzpatrick, *Tanzania, Zanzibar and Pemba* (Lonely Planet Publications, August 1999), 174.
22 Hamo Sassoon, 'The Coastal Town of Jumba La Mtwana', *12 Kenya Past and Present* 2 (1980), 13.

23 Richard Wilding, 'Panels, Pillars and Posterity: Ancient Tombs on the North Kenyan Coast, A Preliminary Study' (Mombasa, *Fort Jesus Occasional Papers* No. 6, 1988), 6.
24 Neville Chittick, 'Relics of the Past in the Region of Dar-es-Salaam, in Dar-es-Salaam City, Port and Region', in *Tanganyika Notes and Records* No. 71 (1970), 65.

18th century (at Kunduchi). Hamo Sassoon speculates that the reason for the pillars 'seems to have been to display the fine porcelain bowls with which the dead person was honoured, perhaps even in those days making it more difficult for thieves to steal them'.[25]

Examples of more ornate such tombs are the Bowl Arcade Dome Tomb at Siu and the bowl frieze on the pillar tomb at Mambrui referred to earlier. At Siu, 'the exterior walls are richly decorated in Chinese Blue and White bowls inset in square coffer arcade panelling [which has over a hundred niches]. There are also bowls set into the dome'.[26]

25 Hamo Sassoon, *Kunduchi: A Guide to the Ruins at Kunduchi* (Dar es Salaam, Ministry of Community Development and National Culture, 1966), 2.
26 Richard Wilding, 'Panels, Pillars and Posterity: Ancient Tombs on the North Kenyan Coast, A Preliminary Study'

Pillar tombs may be categorized as peculiar to the East African coast. But the practice of adorning tombs with porcelain was much wider spread. It is to be found across the whole of the Indian Ocean littoral.

In Indonesia, examples may still be seen in Java. One such prominent tomb is that of Sunan Gunung Jati, one of the most senior of the Nine Saints of Islam in Java. His 16th century CE tomb in the foothills of Mt. Ciremai outside the city of Cirebon is a major pilgrimage site. The exterior walls of the tomb are covered extensively with embedded porcelain bowls and plates.

The direct source of the practice of decorating tombs on the East African coast was,

(Mombasa, *Fort Jesus Occasional Papers* No. 6, 1988), 7.

however, more likely Persia. The import of glazed ware may also have brought with it Persian uses of it. There had been no prior tradition of this practice on tombs on the East African coast. The practice may have moved from the decoration of mosques to the tombs themselves.

In Persia, mosques were embellished with both inlay work and ceramics, and the practice in East Africa of using Chinaware may have originated from there. The 15th century CE Small Domed Mosque at Kilwa 'has glazed Islamic bowls set into the plasterwork of its domes and vaults. Other bowls and tiles were arranged around the *mihrab*. These valuable ceramics were among the luxury goods Kilwa's merchants acquired through

the Indian Ocean trade and sometimes used to embellish their buildings.'[27]

Moon postulates that the Small Domed Mosque at Kilwa may have been a funerary mosque, and it is possible that such decoration in this and other funerary mosques may have influenced the introduction of a similar practice on the pillar tombs.

Schoppert, Sosrowardoyo, and Damais, in their consideration of mosques in Java on the opposite side of the Indian Ocean several thousand miles away, refer (in addition to tombs) to mosques with porcelain decoration. They write, 'Islam found its way to Java through the trading ports of the North Coast. The famous mosque of Demak is reckoned to be Java's oldest. In its walls are found Vietnamese ceramics which must have been specially commissioned; the shapes are

Photos by Villoo Nowrojee

Coral blocks from Jumba la Mtwana, Kongo Mosque, and Mnarani on display at the Gedi Museum.

27 Karen Moon, *Kilwa Kisiwani: Ancient Port City of the East African Coast* (Dar es Salaam, Government of Tanzania, 2005), 25–26.

16

derived from the conventions of Javanese woodcarving and brickwork. The use of ceramics rather than stone is likely to have been in imitation of the mosques of Persia.'[28]

The Small Domed Mosque at Kilwa and the Demak Mosque in Java both shared a common decorative practice, and each had contacts with a common Islamic religious and shipping centre, Persia.

Robinson states that 'this [Persian] custom which was copied by the Arabs and native Swahili population is attributed to the Shirazi (Persian) colonists.'[29]

As Wilding notes, 'The only place in Islamic Africa where pottery bowls were used as a regular form of architectural decoration is on the East African coast. The Persian flavour of this

behaviour suggests strong Persian ties in the Islamic culture of East Africa.'[30] He also considers that, in view of the fact that 'there is no pre−13th century monument on the North Kenya coast with ceramic bowls inset and the practice show[ing] no signs of having continued after the 18th century',[31] this use of pottery 'appears to coincide chronologically and spatially with the Shirazi distribution and social predominance on the East African coast'.[32]

The National Museum in Dar es Salaam, in its section on Kilwa, confirms the Persian connection. On a display of ceramics still embedded in a large masonry fragment, it notes: 'In the 15th Century small Islamic bowls or blue and white Chinese porcelain were inset in many vaults in the Kilwa area. These three bowls are from Persia and were

found at Kilwa and Songo Mnara.'

Over time, the Persian ware came to be replaced by Chinese plates and bowls. At Shee Umuro, on the Kenya coast north of Lamu and close to the Somali border, there are both Persian and Chinese bowls embedded in the obelisks of its pillar tomb.[33] These might date to the 14th century CE. But 'by the fifteenth century the amount of Chinese porcelain in use had considerably increased at the expense of Islamic wares'.[34]

While the centuries-old connections of Java with the islands and coast of eastern Africa might also be a factor to be kept in mind, and while there was undoubted cultural influence from Java and Sumatra,[35] it is more likely

28 Peter Schoppert, Tara Sosrowardoyo, and Soedarmadji Damais, *Java Style* (London, Thames & Hudson, 1997), 21.
29 Arthur E. Robinson, 'Notes on Saucer and Bowl Decorations on Houses, Mosques and Temples', *Tanganyika Notes and Records* No. 10 (December 1940), 79, 84.

30 Richard Wilding, 'The Ceramics of the Lamu Archipelago' (1977), PhD thesis, University of Nairobi, 557gg.
31 Ibid.
32 Ibid.

33 Thomas H. Wilson, 'Conservation of the Ancient Architecture of the Kenya Coast' (1982), 14, in *Kenya Past and Present* 7, 9.
34 John E. G. Sutton, *The East African Coast: An Historical and Archaeological Review* (Dar es Salaam, Historical Association of Tanzania / EA Publishing House, 1966), 12.
35 James Hornell, 'Indonesian Influence

that this particular practice of the use of porcelain was taken by both Indonesia and East Africa from a common source, Persia, rather than from each other. The research so far speaks little of the exchange of Islamic traditions or practice between Indonesia and East Africa, and 'there is no evidence of Indonesians trading on the Swahili Coast later than the thirteenth century CE...'.[36] The similar use of ceramics on monastery walls in Thailand also point to the common Persian connections,[37] as there are so far no known direct connections between Thailand and East Africa.

The Indian Ocean by its huge littoral simultaneously provided both mobility and stability in trade over millennia. Thus it was that Chinese porcelain decorated mosques in East Africa centuries before it finally travelled in substantial quantities to Europe in the 16th century onwards.[38]

It is also likely that wealthy Muslims returning from the Hajj were evoking on their own tombs what they had seen on ornate tombs during their travels in other Muslim lands, where rich inlay work often decorated such tombs.

on East African Culture' (1934), *LXIV Jo. Royal Anthropological Institute*, 305.
36 Mervyn Brown, 'Some Historical Links Between Tanzania and Madagascar' (1976), 79–80, T*anzanian Notes and Records* 49, 53. For a further discussion of Indonesian influences (which discussion, in Sutton's then view, 'remains unsatisfactory'), see 'The Indonesian Problem' in John E. G. Sutton, *The East African Coast: An Historical and Archaeological Review* (Dar es Salaam, Historical Association of Tanzania / EA Publishing House, 1966), 8–9.

37 Richard Wilding, 'The Ceramics of the Lamu Archipelago' (1977), PhD thesis, University of Nairobi, 557gg.
38 R. J. Charleston (ed.), *English Porcelain 1745–1850* (London, Ernest Benn/University of Toronto, 1965), 17.

Inlay work was not available on the East African coast, but the appearance of some inlay designs could be approximated by a plate of fine blue china.

Wilding too considers such decoration as following the examples of other Muslim lands. He considers the practice here as an East African variant 'of the widespread Islamic (but most characteristically, Persian) practice of decorating buildings with mosaics and tiles'.[39] He continues, 'There are numerous examples in Islamic architecture of the use of the Sassanian sun disc symbol or a simple circular boss, plaque or emphales in positions directly analogous to those occupied by ceramic bowls in the East African mosques. It would seem this

was a regional modification of the common architectural motif.'[40]

From a decorative practice in funerary mosques to the decoration of tombs themselves was a likely next step. More so when it conferred or continued to confer status, even posthumously.

PROTECTIVE PURPOSES

There was another consideration as well. Wilson adverts to it in his examination of 'step-ends' on many of the coastal tombs. 'Step-ends may be seen on the corners of houses in other areas of the Islamic world, where in addition to their obvious decorative appeal they are thought to ward off evil spirits. On the tombs, then, they

might have been intended to discourage evil spirits. The imported ceramics often found decorating the superstructures of tombs might have served a similar protective function.'[41]

This aspect is also one of several considered by Robinson in an early examination of the possible functions.[42]

Writing in 1940, Robinson stated, 'In recent years travellers in Upper Egypt, East Africa and the East have described a practice of affixing earthenware plates, saucers or bowls in the walls above the doors of houses, mosques, tombs, etc.' He viewed it as one 'which seems to have

39 Richard Wilding, 'The Ceramics of the Lamu Archipelago' (1977), PhD thesis, University of Nairobi, 557ff.

40 Ibid. 557gg.

41 Thomas H. Wilson, 'Conservation of the Ancient Architecture of the Kenya Coast' (1982), 14, in *Kenya Past and Present* 7, 13.
42 Arthur E. Robinson, 'Notes on Saucer and Bowl Decorations on Houses, Mosques and Temples', *Tanganyika Notes and Records* No. 10 (December 1940), 79.

developed during a comparatively recent period'.

The observation should, if at all valid, be restricted to Egypt, to the absence of which custom in that country around 1835 he makes a comparison. In respect of East Africa, all the archaeological evidence shows that here this was a very old tradition in mosques and on tombs. In East Africa, the presence of fine china as a decoration in houses too was already centuries old by the time Robinson was writing.

Robinson reviewed the use of charms and protective objects against the evil eye, in Europe, Egypt, Ethiopia, and the Holy Lands. He then concluded that 'although there are numerous allusions to Djinns (Genii, evil and good) in the Quran, it would appear that the only orthodox preventive against evil is written or spoken prayer' (at 82). This is underscored by the fact that (in contrast to the 'modern' practice of

embedding plates above the outside door) doorways and lintels carved with verses from the Quran had been common for centuries.

While Robinson observed that plate and saucer decorations were sometimes seen over the houses occupied by Hajjis, he stated that he could not remember seeing any evidence of a saucer cult in Syria, Turkey, or North Africa—including northern Egypt and Cairo.

We believe that Robinson erred in viewing the increased use he saw of decorated plates as an isolated cult or practice, instead of as a sign of the greater democratization and wider geographical spread of a very old tradition in Islamic art. He does not mention the type of ceramic the saucer and bowls that he saw were. But it is necessary to take into account that cheaper ceramics came into those very markets in large numbers at the same time (around the third quarter of the 19th century), and from the very same sources in Western Europe that had then reached the East African coast and the Muslim lands of the Indian Ocean with these products.

On the purposes, Robinson finally offers no firm conclusion: 'I cannot suggest at present any purpose for the bowls than that of a decoration or a permanent votary offering to the deceased...I expect the present generation (both in East Africa and elsewhere) regard them as charms, whatever be their origin.'[43]

There is some corroboration of this in a long consideration of uses by Dr. Linda Wiley Donley-Reid.[44] Rather than the assumption that such bowls were used to serve food to the wealthy, as Chittick (1974, 244) proposed, she posits that 'porcelain and glazed wares were used more for decoration than for serving food. Collections [of porcelain] were made and displayed in the many plaster wall niches found in the eighteenth and nineteenth century northern Swahili houses.'[45]

Her broader findings and conclusion are that porcelain was used as a protective charm within Swahili society.[46] Like Robinson (whom Donley-Reid does not mention at all), she refers to Middle Eastern practices. However, it is the evidence she found in Lamu of porcelain shards in infant burials, and of porcelain shards with holes in them suggesting their use as protective pendants, that principally led her to her conclusion. In support, she cites Mathew ('probable...had some magical significance')[47] and Ingrams ('broken plates on Swahili graves were not for decoration but for protection against "devils"').[48]

Porcelain was regarded, in this use, as a medium to 'absorb' the 'evil eye'. Kalandar Khan writes, 'The Waswahili display China plates to protect them from the "evil eye" or *Hasidi*, as well as anyone who enters the house. In contrast to the Nubians, the Waswahili believe that the ceramic ware absorbs rather than reflects the "evil eye". The imported ceramic ware on the *Zidaka* are thus a form of protection from the "evil eye", as the Waswahili believe that the "evil eye" is able to cause great harm and even death and hence the ceramic ware absorbs the malevolent spirits and protects the owner of the house from any harm.'[49]

Though this was more

---

43 Ibid. 87.
44 Linda Wiley Donley-Reid, 'The Social Uses of Swahili Space and Objects' (1984), PhD thesis, Cambridge University (Chapter 8, 'Imported Porcelain and Glazed Wares').

45 Ibid. 313.
46 Ibid. 315.
47 Rev. Gervase Mathew, *The Culture of the East African Coast in the Seventeenth and Eighteenth Centuries* (1956), 68.

48 W. H. Ingrams, *Zanzibar: Its History and Its People* (London, H. F. & G. Witherby, 1931), 242.
49 Kalandar Kamal Khan, *The Swahili Architecture of Lamu, Kenya: Oral Tradition and Space* (Saarbruken, Lambert Academic Publishing, 2010).

usual, the warding off of the 'evil eye' was practiced in Nubia additionally through the use of shiny metal plates that 'deflected' the evil eye. Mahgoub writes of the Nubia that china plates were placed at the entrance of homes to indicate that the man of the house was alive and 'also protected the residents of the house from the harm of the evil eye of strangers. By distracting the attention of the strangers to these decorations and objects, the plates and decorations protected the inhabitants of the house from the evil eye.'[50]

Freeman-Grenville also considered the uses to which these Chinese ceramics were put. 'It is possible,' he wrote of the use of porcelain plates in mosques, 'that this form had a magical purpose, but later the intention seems to have been no more than decorative. This is borne out by the decoration of a small ante-chamber in the Palace of Dongo ya Mnara, near Kilwa Kisiwani, with more than 3,009 plates inset into cavities in the roof; and again by the two lines in *Al-Inkishafi* ["now wildlings birds nestle" quoted earlier].'[51]

'But,' he goes on, 'was the original intention solely decorative? In the Pangani District Book a writer records how at the burial in 1931 of Zumbe Diwani Simba of Mkwaja [in Tanganyika], porcelain plates were ceremoniously broken over his grave. There is a considerable body of evidence of a cult of the dead in which offerings of food and incense are placed in shards of pottery or porcelain at important tombs: at least fifty examples are known to me.'[52]

50 Yasser Osman Moharam Mahgoub, 'The Nubian Experience: A Study of the Social and Cultural Meanings of Architecture', D.Arch. dissertation, University of Michigan, 1990. See too Makokha Kusimba (1994) below, who also notes these Nubian and Nigerian practices.

51 G. S. P. Freeman-Grenville, 'Chinese Porcelain in Tanganyika', *Tanganyika Notes and Records* No. 41, (December 1955), 65.

52 Ibid. Freeman-Grenville also mentions similar beliefs in Mozambique (circa 1593 CE), Persia (13th century CE), and

Whether, during those periods, these were syncretic practices attaching to Islam as it established itself alongside traditional beliefs in Eastern Africa or were existing social practices or social imports needs to be re-examined.[53]

Different purposes and uses in different parts of the region emerge. On a review of the material, we may conclude that domestic use, decoration, the warding off of the evil eye, uses in burial rituals, and the announcement of status have all played a part in the use of ceramics in East Africa.

As Status

Fine china has everywhere always been regarded with the highest respect. We ought not to be surprised at its use in architecture such as tombs and mosques. We must remember that 'when Chinese porcelain was first introduced into the Mongol Empire.

Europe in the Middle Ages it was regarded as a magical, or quasi-magical, substance and was credited with extraordinary properties.'[54] 'Asian porcelain was even termed "white gold" and thought to possess magical properties.'[55]

That such decoration also indicated status may additionally be gathered from the use of such decoration in other Islamic countries. In Indonesia, on certain palace (*kraton*) outbuildings in Java, Chinaware is extensively embedded on their exteriors. An example is in the palace grounds of the Kraton Kanoman, built in 1677, in Ceribon, Java.[56]

On the East African coast, early 14th and 15th century CE ceramics from China, for both domestic

53 See Timothy Insoll, 'Archaeology and the Reconstruction of Religious Identity in Africa (and Beyond)' (2004), *Azania XXXIX*, 195, 197–200.

54 R. J. Charleston (ed.), *English Porcelain 1745–1850* (London, Ernest Benn / University of Toronto, 1965), 17.
55 Kan Shuyi, *Inspired By Japan and China: The Egawa Collection of European Ceramics* (Singapore, Asian Civilizations Museum, 2011), 10.
56 Peter Schoppert, Tara Sosrowardoyo, and Soedarmadji Damais, *Java Style* (London, Thames & Hudson, 1997), 46.

and funerary use, have been found at Gedi, Ungwana, and Ngomeni. Examples of these are on display at the Fort Jesus Museum, Mombasa, and at the museum at Gedi. Other prominent examples are from Kilwa (from the Tombs of the Kilwa Sultans and the Malindi Mosque Cemetery there), generously displayed at the National Museum, Dar es Salaam.[57]

OTHER USES

The varied uses to which Chinaware was put, and echoes of those uses in other regions, are summarized by Makokha Kusimba thus: 'Indeed a large proportion of imported ceramics was inserted into the ceilings and walls of domestic buildings, mosques, mosque *mihrabs* and tombs, and into water cisterns. Although ethnographically the practice has been observed in Nubia and Nigeria, archaeologically it is said to be confined to the East African Coast.'[58]

Another use of these ceramics is the placing of plates at the bottom of the *birika*, the water cistern. This too has been continuously documented. Donley-Reid found 18th century blue-and-white Chinese bowls at the bottom of the *birika* during archaeological excavations in Lamu and Pate.[59] As did Wilding, with both much older and more recent bowls.[60] The practice continues. Prof. Abdul Sheriff a few years ago noted one of these plates inlaid at the bottom of a storage basin of ablution water in Lamu. He was informed that small fish were kept in the basin to eat mosquito larvae. However, to prevent the fish from dying when the water level got too low, the plate was inlaid to ensure that there would always be some water.[61] The photograph in the Abungus' *Lamu* best illustrates this use of the plates.[62]

57 See also Richard Wilding, *The Far Eastern Pottery Collection of the National Museum at Dar-es-Salaam* (Nairobi, British Institute of History and Archaeology of Eastern Africa, 1971).

58 Makokha Kusimba, 'Chinese Ceramics in the Fort Jesus Museum Collection' (1994), 26, *Kenya Past and Present* 55, citing Caroline Sassoon, *Chinese Porcelain Marks from Coastal Sites in Kenya: Aspects of Trade in the Indian Ocean, XIV-XIX Centuries* (1978), BAR International Series (Supplementary), 43, 3.

59 Linda Wiley Donley-Reid, 'The Social Uses of Swahili Space and Objects' (1984), PhD thesis, Cambridge University, 323.

60 Richard Wilding, 'The Ceramics of the Lamu Archipelago' (1977), PhD thesis, University of Nairobi, 557jj.

61 Communication from Prof. Abdul Sheriff, 30 August 2008.

62 George and Lorna Abungu, *Lamu: Kenya's Enchanted Island* (New York, Rizzoli International Publications, 2009), 81.

THE TRADE IN CHINESE GOODS WITH EAST AFRICA

ALTHOUGH CHINESE ceramics, both fine and utilitarian, had been received and used on the East African coast for several centuries earlier, 'The Chinese trade was carried by Arabs and Indians, and it was only during the Fifteenth century that Chinese ships actually reached the East Coast of Africa. In 1417 and 1421 they visited Malindi, and it was there that they found the first famous giraffe ever to be seen in China.'[1]

These were the visits during the epic sea voyages under the great Chinese Admiral Zheng He between 1405 and 1433.[2] Hamo Sassoon refers to them, stating that 'a great Chinese fleet of 62 ships and 37,000 men did pay a diplomatic call at Malindi in 1417'.[3] Caroline Sassoon notes that 'although there is mention of Chinese ships visiting Malindi between 1417 and 1422, they normally sailed only to India and Malacca, and the other seamen continued to carry the trade'[4] and 'there is, unfortunately, no record of the naval ships [in 1417 and 1421] engaging in trade'.[5]

Soon after the last of these major voyages of the great admiral, his patron the Emperor Zhu Di died in 1424. His successors stopped all voyages, and China entered a long period of xenophobia and embargoes on foreign trade.[6] It is not surprising that 'in the years that followed, the great trade in porcelain was probably conducted almost wholly

1 Caroline Sassoon, *Chinese Porcelain Marks from Coastal Sites in Kenya: Aspects of Trade in the Indian Ocean XIV–XIX Centuries* (1978), BAR International Series (Supplementary), 43, 2.

2 See Admiral Zheng He, *Exhibition at Fort Jesus, Mombasa,* September–October 2005; J. J. L. Duyvendak, *China's Discovery of Africa* (London, 1949); the re-introductory work by Gavin Menezies, *1421: The Year China Discovered the World* (London, Bantam Press, 2002); Cynthia Hunter K'I-lin, 'The Celestial Giraffe', *Kenya Past and Present* No. 10 (1979), 29; *The Economist,* 14 January 2006, 80.
3 Hamo Sassoon, 'The Coastal Town of Jumba la Mtwana' (1980), 12, *Kenya Past and Present* 2, 13.
4 Caroline Sassoon, *Chinese Porcelain in Fort Jesus* (Mombasa, National Museums

of Kenya, 1975) n.p.
5 Caroline Sassoon, *Chinese Porcelain Marks from Coastal Sites in Kenya: Aspects of Trade in the Indian Ocean XIV–XIX Centuries* (1978), BAR International Series (Supplementary), 43, 2.
6 Gavin Menezies, *1421: The Year China Discovered the World* (London, Bantam Press, 2002), 81–85.

through middlemen in India and in South Arabia'.[7]

Freeman-Grenville also observes (apart from the embassies of 1417 and 1431 [sic]) that G. F. Hourani in his standard work[8] also noted 'that trade between the East Coast and China was entirely conducted through entrepôts, without direct contact'.[9]

'In Duarte Barbosa,'[10] Freeman-Grenville continues, 'we read of Indian merchants of Kutch and the Kathiawar coast who brought goods from China to sell to Arabs who came from Siraf in the Persian Gulf and from Oman, and who themselves sold to the Arab *nakhoda* or sea captains,

who came, as they still do today, in their dhows on the north-east monsoon.'[11]

It is important to note that at one time this aspect led to the presence of East African agents at the opposite eastern end of the Indian Ocean, at those ports of contact between the Indian and Chinese merchants. Freeman-Grenville adds:

'Both Kilwa and Mombasa maintained trade agents in Malacca as late as 1515[12] and probably this was no small part of their business, in exchange for East African ivory, which China was already importing in quantity by the 9th Century, and in all likelihood long before.'[13] [14]

7 G. S. P. Freeman-Grenville, 'Some Problems of East African Coinage: From Early Times to 1890', *Tanganyika Notes and Records* No. 53 (October 1959), 250, 253.
8 George Hourani, *Arab Seafaring in the Indian Ocean in Ancient and Mediaeval Times* (Princeton, Princeton University Press, 1951; 1995).
9 G. S. P. Freeman-Grenville, 'Chinese Porcelain in Tanganyika', *Tanganyika Notes and Records* No. 41 (December 1955), 63.
10 *The Book of Duarte Barbosa* (London, Hakluyt Society, 1918).

11 G. S. P. Freeman-Grenville, 'Chinese Porcelain in Tanganyika', *Tanganyika Notes and Records* No. 41 (December 1955), 63.
12 *The Suma Oriental of Tome Pires*, circa 1515–1517 (2 Volumes, The Hakluyt Society, 1944) Vol. I, 14.
13 G. S. P. Freeman-Grenville, 'Some Recent Archaeological Work on the Tanganyikan Coast', *Man*, Vol. LVIII, July 1958, 108.
14 G. S. P. Freeman-Grenville, 'Some Problems of East African Coinage: From Early Times to 1890', *Tanganyika Notes*

Thus Chinaware illustrates an important part of the Indian Ocean connections between the Malacca islands, India, Persia, Oman, and Arabia and the East African coast that our history abundantly contains.

Chinaware thus continued to be imported by the East African coast by the above routes.

In research in both Kenya and India, Donley-Reid found 'The same variety of Chinese wares commonly found on the eastern coast of Africa was also present in the towns on the Gujarat coast, the area known to have served as an entrepôt for the China porcelain trade. A photo was taken of a collection of Chinese porcelain in a Bohra's house in Mandvi (Figure 73). The Bohra said that this was the type of ware that his family sold in East Africa during difficult times in Kutch. Some of his relatives own and operate a general store in Lamu today.'[15]

In the century that followed, the availability of Chinese ware also came from another source. Robinson citing Pearce (1920)[16] wrote, 'It would appear that Chinese artisans were sent from China to Persia as late as the seventeenth century where they established a factory under the patronage of Shah Abbas. These Chinese artisans made bowls of imitation Chinese porcelain and forged the ancient marks after copying the style.'[17]

THE DECLINE OF CHINESE IMPORTS

As the 1800s began, further changes took place, both in

and Records No. 53 (October 1959), 250 at 253.

15 Linda Wiley Donley-Reid, 'The Social Uses of Swahili Space and Objects' (1984), PhD thesis, Cambridge University, 319.
16 Major Francis Barrow Pearce, Zanzibar: The Island Metropolis of Eastern Africa (London, Unwin, 1920).
17 Arthur E. Robinson, 'Notes on Saucer and Bowl Decorations on Houses, Mosques and Temples', Tanganyika Notes and Records No. 10 (December 1940), 85.

our region and in China, which brought even the reduced imports to an end. Three major factors were responsible.

During this period, the military control of the Indian Ocean moved to new imperial powers. In the early 16th century CE, soon after the passage of Vasco da Gama around the Cape of Good Hope, the Portuguese had established naval supremacy first over the Arabian Sea and then over the vaster waters from Mozambique to the Straits of Malacca. But though Portuguese interests were long present on the East African coast, trade patterns there did not change significantly. It was only later, in the period before and after 1800, when British and Dutch rivals consolidated rule over subject lands and decisively established their own supremacy in their re-spective spheres of influence in the Indian Ocean, that trade patterns as well as cultural patterns were significantly affected.

Several factors brought this about. Firstly, when the pattern of trade in Indian goods altered, the pattern of trade in Chinese goods in East Africa also had to alter, because (as set out above) East Africa's substantial trading connections in Chinese goods were with India, and not with China itself. This was a geographical and historical development arising out of what K. M. Pannikar has pointed out:

'India's trade, unlike that of China, was at all times predominantly maritime. In China, trade followed the caravan route, the route of camels. Chinese economy was therefore continental. India on the other hand, her land mass closed on three sides by mountains, had her trade routes mainly along sea routes. When these sea routes came to be controlled by the European powers, the economy of India began to be dependent to a large extent on the foreign merchants. When in the 18th and 19th centuries commerce developed on a world scale, the emphasis in India shifted from the interior to the coast, and the great cities of Calcutta, Bombay and Madras began to take the place of Delhi, Agra and Allahabad.'[18]

As noted earlier, trade had continued mainly through India and South Arabia. Now, in the 1800s, India, Muscat, and Bandar Abbas became centres of trans-shipments of European wares, India for the produce of the English potteries, and the others for Dutch and French ceramics. For the latter, there was a big market in the Gulf, and their East African market became a part of the Arab trade with East Africa.

As their empires expanded, English and Dutch control enabled them to dictate the

18 K. M. Pannikar, *Geographical Factors in Indian History* (Bombay, Bharatiya Vidya Bhavan, 1959), 86–87.

sources and direction of trade in the Indian Ocean. Items that could be supplied from their metropolitan producers began to dominate its markets there, while imports from the traditional Indian Ocean suppliers (including China through India) increasingly declined and, in respect of some items such as fine china and fine Indian cloth, almost disappeared from the general market.

Secondly, the consolidation of British and Dutch power in India, the Arabian Peninsula, the East Indies, and particularly the East African coast also altered what was socially to be esteemed, and what would constitute appropriate indicators of social status. Oil paintings, prints, photographs increasingly, and furniture of a different kind all moved to displace china as the sole decoration or mark of affluence in a house.

THE DECLINE: SOCIAL FACTORS

A further factor accompanied the rise and consolidation of empire. This was the increasing arrival in the colonies of the families of officials from the metropolitan centres in Western Europe. This development led to a major shift in the social arbiters of taste—from the families of the nobles on the East African coast to the official families of the new colonial rulers, latterly the British.[19]

An example of the impact of this factor on social artifacts is the dinner service of the late 1800s of the Sultans

19 Pearce records a gift from Queen Victoria to Sultan Sayyid Said in the 1840s of 'a splendid silver-gilt tea service. For political reasons connected with his Omani possessions and the financial and other demands of his Wahabi neighbours to the north, Sultan Said sent [it] at dead of night back to the British Consulate for safe keeping. What eventually happened to this gift history does not record' (*Zanzibar*, 125).

of Zanzibar, carrying the Sultanate crest. These can be seen in the Beit-el-Ajaib Museum, Zanzibar, the Palace Museum, Zanzibar, and Fort Jesus Museum, Mombasa. The pattern is modelled on, and therefore imposes the tastes of, a Western court suitably modified downwards for what was viewed as sub-royalty.

It would have been more befitting, and infinitely more pleasing to the eye, had the dinner set displayed simply the red flag of Zanzibar or the individual *tughra* (pronounced 'toora'; also spelled *tuğra* or *toughra*)[20] of the particular Sultan. 'The *tugra* [sic], an Ottoman creation, was the royal or imperial monogram, the calligraphic emblem of the reigning monarch or sultan. It incorporated his name, his

20 *Islamic Calligraphy* (Singapore, Asian Civilizations Museum, 2008), 7.

The *tughra* of Sultan of Zanzibar Sayyid Khalifa bin Harub, who ruled from 1911 to 1960.

patronymic, and the phrase "the ever victorious". Each sultan chose his personal *tugra* immediately on accession and used it throughout his reign, though it could be enhanced by further ornament.'[21]

The decision not to use the Omani flag or the Sultan's personal *tughra* on the dinner service was a social judgment

21 *Traces of the Calligrapher: Islamic Calligraphy in Practice, c. 1600–1900*, Exhibition, Asia Society, New York, 2008–2009.

and not a political choice, because the latter choice had already been made in favour of the use of the *tughra* on all government laws (where it already appeared). The choice instead of a derivative coat of arms from the College of Arms in England, which was even a bit Ruritanian, spoke of poor design in plate as well as heraldry.

Another factor in the decline of Chinaware on the East African coast was the impact of the expanding Western European powers on China itself and in the internal events there.

In the first part of the 19th century, and again in the middle years (1853), factories in China were destroyed by civil war and rebellion. Caroline Sassoon records, 'It took over twenty years for

them to be rebuilt and for production to start again. During that time European "china" had invaded the markets. These were products which were factory produced and mechanically decorated, often with copies of popular Chinese designs such as the character *shou*, the "chrysanthemum" and scroll, and chinoiserie such as the "willow pattern".[22]

Copies were first made of Chinese designs and motifs, often imperfectly. Kan Shuyi in *Inspired by Japan and China*, her consideration of the impact of China and Japan on European ceramics, notes: 'Imaginary visions of the East shaped European designs, resulting in landscapes, people, and animals that the Chinese and the Japanese would not have recognized... Chinese- and Japanese-style motifs appear on wares with European shapes...While the original inspiration may be in some sense Asian, the end results were often creative responses to local needs and tastes.'[23]

But manufacturers in Western Europe were not only seeking to imitate and reproduce designs and motifs. They were also searching for chemical formulae to reproduce the materials of Chinaware, in particular porcelain. This was finally deciphered and applied first at factories in Meissen in Germany and then in England and France.

Copies of Chinese ware, and English copies of German copies of such ware, all entered a highly competitive market, providing the much sought after, very expensive porcelain, as well as the utilitarian and cheap blue and white.

The effect of these several factors was as Caroline Sassoon concluded: 'The supremacy of Chinese

22 Caroline Sassoon, *Chinese Porcelain in Fort Jesus* (Mombasa, National Museums of Kenya, 1975) n.p.

23 Kan Shuyi, *Inspired By Japan and China: The Egawa Collection of European Ceramics* (Singapore, Asian Civilizations Museum, 2011), 19.

porcelain had ended after nearly a thousand years of dominance.'[24]

During this period, however, there was in Zanzibar another way by which Chinaware was acquired. Pieces were sent 'as a present to Seyyid Said by His Imperial Majesty the Emperor of China, and contained varieties of foodstuffs highly esteemed as delicacies by the Chinese. Seyyid Barghash added to their number other bowls and jars of similar pattern by purchase from China.'[25]

Shipping patterns also changed in the second half of the 19th century CE. Prior to that, 'Most of the English china came via Bombay, since direct trade between Britain and East Africa, except in muskets, was slight for most of Saiyid Said's reign [1806–1856] and stopped completely between 1848 and 1855.'[26] The trans-shipment from Bombay was, as has been noted, also the route for fine ware from China.

But in the next decade two key factors wrought changes that brought European china directly to East Africa. These were the opening of the Suez Canal in 1869 and the development of steamships, which took commercial goods to empire and world markets in half the time of the fastest sailing vessels. These two factors combined to multiply several-fold the goods from Western Europe thereafter available in East African markets.

'European china was, of course, well known all over the Indian Ocean by the end of the eighteenth century and was in use in Zanzibar in the 1820s. Cups and plates even reached the Kabaka of Buganda in the middle of the eighteenth century.'[27] This is also reflected in the 1893 report sent by Sir Gerald Portal to the Foreign Secretary in London, where he states, 'In this connection, I would remark that in Uganda there does exist already a distinct demand for European commodities, more especially for such articles as cotton cloths of the best qualities, boots and articles of clothing.'[28] But all this, according to Kirkman, 'was something exceptional'. In contrast, this ware was now (1893) arriving as part of a regular trade and in large volumes.

The invading pottery came mainly from Holland and England. James de Vere Allen records the change in respect of Lamu. 'In the early Nineteenth Century Lamu continued to import mainly Chinese pieces. Then as her

24 Caroline Sassoon, *Chinese Porcelain in Fort Jesus* (Mombasa, National Museums of Kenya, 1975) n.p.
25 R. H. Crofton, *Zanzibar Affairs: 1914–1933* (London, Francis Edwards, 1953), 49.

26 James Kirkman, *Fort Jesus* (Nairobi, Oxford University Press, 1974), 121, citing C. S. Nicholls, *The Swahili Coast* (London, 1971), 335–338.

27 Ibid.
28 *Africa*, No. 2 (1894), 29; M. F. Hill, *Permanent Way*, Vol. I (Nairobi, East African Railways & Harbours, 1949), 121.

decline set in and the pattern of world markets changed, this was mainly replaced by pottery from the cheaper kilns of Europe—France, Germany, Belgium and Holland in particular.'[29]

These are the plates that came to prevail on the East African coast, and in Zanzibar in particular, that we now collectively call Zanzibar plates.

Prof. John Middleton, in writing of the Swahili, also sets out the progression from early Islamic pottery to fine china to Zanzibar plates: Chinese porcelain (plates, jars, and bowls) 'of the 14th and 15th centuries were largely of sea-green celadon ware;

in the 16th century blue and white porcelain became more popular. Glazed earthenware, the yellow-and-green *sgraffito* ware that was the universal Islamic pottery of the late Middle Ages, was also imported from Persia. Other imported pottery included heavy Chinese glossy blue, green and turquoise bowls; in the 17th and 18th centuries Portuguese and Spanish blue and white pottery became fashionable, followed by painted Dutch and other trade ware.'[30]

THE DECLINE OF LAMU

In the early period of this latter commerce (the 1860s and 1870s),[31] these imports were received at all the

main ports on the East African coast, Lamu being a major recipient. But soon, several events contributed to propel Zanzibar to unrivalled dominance. The move in 1856 of the more permanent and formal siting of the Sultanate in Zanzibar altered Zanzibar's political and mercantile standing significantly, to its advantage. Diplomatic missions arrived there.

Numerous merchants of all trades set up shop in the city. Western shipping connections opened up, and foreign trade increased dramatically. 'The political power was there, the foreign consuls and agents congregated there, and in time Zanzibar's policy of centralizing all imports and exports through her own warehouses left Lamu far behind. The inadequacy of Lamu's port facilities for the steamship age and the operations of the Witu Sultanate of Swahililand, which harassed

29 James de Vere Allen, *Lamu* (Nairobi, Kenya Museum Society, 1972), 23. In referring to the replacement of Chinese ware, Donley-Reid cites Allen but does not refer to the produce of the 'cheaper kilns of Europe'. Instead she identifies the 'most common' of the replacements to be 'a Dutch pearlware, 1795–1815'. This is not the period of which Allen is speaking ('as the decline of Lamu set in'), nor the goods, and she makes no mention of these later Maastricht and similar wares that came to be the principal replacements.

30 John Middleton, *The World of the Swahili: An African Mercantile Civilization* (New Haven, Yale University Press, 1992), 206.
31 James Kirkman, at least in the Fort Jesus excavations, found the largest numbers of the earliest plates from Western Europe to be of manufacture from the third quarter of the century: James Kirkman, *Fort Jesus* (Oxford, Clarendon Press, 1974), 121.

Lamu's mainland estates, were contributory causes to her decline. Her revenues, based as they were on the twin supports of mainland agriculture and maritime trade, could not survive such a two-pronged attack.'[32]

The import trade thus decisively moved to Zanzibar, making it then the central point of distribution for the whole East African coast, even though Lamu remained an important outpost for Zanzibar. By the end of the century, Lamu was a net importer from Zanzibar and even from Mombasa. The principal source of the plates for the whole coast had by then become Zanzibar.

32 James de Vere Allen, *Lamu Town: A Guide* (Lamu, National Museums of Kenya, 1977), 9.

SUBSTITUTES FROM EUROPE

THESE TRENDS coincided with the decline noted above in the production and availability of fine ware from China. The result was that in major social settings replacements had to be found for the unavailable fine china. A substitution was needed in homes, as well as in mosques and on tombs in funerary decoration.

'The more important Swahili, when dead, were placed in tombs adorned with porcelain bowls, and devout builders mounted them around the *mihrabs* of their mosques. This practice continued up to the end of the 1800s, when European china of inferior quality was used in place of the no longer obtainable Chinese porcelain.'[1]

1 James de Vere Allen, *Lamu Town: A Guide* (Lamu, National Museums of Kenya, 1977).

The expanded uses of the newly available Maastricht-type ware were now beginning to reflect the uses to which fine china had been put in the immediate past centuries.

SUBSTITUTES ON TOMBS AND IN MOSQUES

An example of the use of Zanzibar plates on funerary buildings is on Tomb No. 7 at Kunduchi, Dar es Salaam, Tanzania. 'The design is known as "Caledonia" and it is by Adams of Tunstall, Staffordshire, England. It is dated to about 1830.'[2] Another plate from Kunduchi cemetery (on display at the National Museum in Dar es Salaam) is also a 19th century CE product showing a scene from a stag hunt. It is in a rich rose colour and is of English or German manufacture.

Another example may be

seen in Zanzibar city on the tomb of Sheikh Ahmed bin Sumeit. Sayyid Ahmed bin Sumeit was a Hadhrami Sunni scholar who had connections with the Comoros. He died in 1943. The inscription on his tomb is in Arabic and Gujarati.[3] In the age-old tradition of paying homage at the tombs of Islamic holy men, followers still 'visit the contemporary tombs of eminent sheikhs, which like those of Sd. Ahmed b. Sumeit and Sh. Abdullah Bakathir, have left a perennial trace in the memory of Sunni Muslims (be they of African, Arab or Indo-Pakistani origin) in East Africa and the Comoro Islands. The former is situated near the Malindi Friday Mosque, inside a small covered structure.'[4] The

small tomb inside the building is decorated with a Zanzibar plate embedded in it.

As in East Africa, so in Java fine china came in time to share space with, or to be superseded by, Dutch and other ceramics. Plates from China may be seen on the tombs in Java, but also visible now are Maastricht-type designs. This is further confirmed by Schoppert and co-authors, who write that 'when pieces of porcelain covering the enclosure break, they are replaced with new pieces brought by well-wishers. Today the porcelains are mostly of European and Japanese origin.'[5] These include Maastricht plates or more recent copies of them.

Like their Chinese predecessors, Zanzibar plates too became, in Alexander's words, 'constituents of the

2 Hamo Sassoon, *Guide to the Ruins at Kunduchi* (Dar es Salaam, Ministry of Community Development and National Culture, 1966).

3 Amina Ameir Issa, 'The Burial of the Elite in Nineteenth Century Zanzibar Stone Town', in Abdul Sheriff (ed.), *The History and Conservation of Zanzibar Stone Town* (London, Department of Archives, Museums and Antiquities, Zanzibar/James Currey, 1995), 67–80.
4 Jean-Claude Penrad, 'The Social Fallout of Individual Death: Graves and Cemeteries in Zanzibar', in Abdul Sheriff (ed.), *The History and Conservation of Zanzibar Stone Town* (London,

Department of Archives, Museums and Antiquities, Zanzibar/James Currey, 1995), 82, at 89, and its photograph Figure 6.2 (ii) at 84.
5 Peter Schoppert, Tara Sosrowardoyo, and Soedarmadji Damais, *Java Style* (London, Thames & Hudson, 1997), 49.

archaeology of Islam in East Africa'.[6]

SUBSTITUTES IN *ZIDAKA*

In East Africa, another social aspect in which similar change from fine china to Maastricht-type plates took place was in regard to long-established patterns in domestic buildings. The wall niches called *zidaka* (also *vidaka*; the singular is *kidaka*) had for long been the setting for Chinese plates and bowls.

Usam Ghaidan in *Lamu: A Study of the Swahili Town*[7] cites further stanzas from *Al-Inkishafi* as evidence of the architectural aspects of this use of china:

*49 Nyumba zao mbake
ziwele tame;
makinda ya popo iyu
wengeme.*

Plate from the Sultan's Palace, Zanzibar. (Cyrus and Jenny Talati Collection.)

Photos © Cyrus and Jenny Talati

6 John Alexander, 'The Archaeological Recognition of Religion: The Examples of Islam in Africa and "Urnfields" in Europe', in B. Burnham and J. Kingsbury (eds.), *Space, Hierarchy and Settlement* (Oxford, British Archaeological Reports, BAR S59), 215.
7 Nairobi, EA Literature Bureau, 1975.

Husikii hisi wala ukeme;
zitanda matandu
walitandiye.
The lighted mansions are
uninhabited,
The young bats cling up
above,
You hear no whispering,
nor shouting,
Spiders crawl over the beds.

50 Madaka ya nyumba ya
zisahani,
sasa walaliye wana wa
nyuni.
Bumu hukoroma kati
nyumbani;
zisiji na kotwe waikaliye.
The wall niches for porcelain in the houses
Are now the resting-places
for nestlings,
Owls hoot within the
house,
Mannikin birds and ducks
dwell within.[8]

8 Sayyid Abdalla bin Ali bin Nasir,
Al-Inkishafi: Catechism of a Soul,
transl. James de Vere Allen (Nairobi,
EA Literature Bureau, 1977), 41; Jan
Knappert, *Four Centuries of Swahili*
Verse: A Literary History NS Anthology
(London, Heinemann Educational,
1979), 127–137.

Ghaidan elaborates on
the place and purpose of the
niches. 'As one traverses the
house away from the court,
niches increase; the last wall
of the inner room is almost
entirely covered by them.
Here, the *zidaka*, as they are
called, take the form of arched
and rectangular niches of
varying proportions and in
most cases, a fixed module...
The reference to porcelain in
zidaka in the early nineteenth
century poem [quoted above],
and information received
from elders in Lamu town,
seem to suggest that the
zidaka were used for display
rather than storage. In the
niches the wife arranged her
showpieces: imported pottery,
bronze artifacts, ornamented
manuscripts, etc.'[9]

9 Usam Ghaidan, *Lamu: A Study of*
the Swahili Town, at 47–48. See also
Ghaidan's Figure 33, a photograph
of a then contemporary (1975) Lamu
interior displaying china on wall shelves,
including Zanzibar plates; and the
illustration of a similar *kidaka*, with
Zanzibar plates, in John Middleton's
The World of the Swahili: An African
Mercantile Civilization (New Haven,
Yale UP, 1992). For further examples
of contemporary *zidaka*, see George

It is necessary to consider
the *zidaka* at this stage, as
they were an integral part of
the use of ceramics in East
Africa. A primary place for
Chinese plates and bowls was
in the niches of the *zidaka* as
opposed to on the walls. The
zidaka's contents signalled that
these were the items cherished
by the owners.

Orme-Smith suggests
another purpose of the *zidaka*:
'They also provide a *trompe*
d'oeil to give the illusion that
the room is larger and the ceil-
ing higher, the use for display
or storage being secondary.'[10]
As the *zidaka* are usually the
last wall, this is a plausible
aspect kept in mind by the
architect of the house, especially as the size of the rooms
and the low ceilings would
benefit from the impression of
additional space.

Romero states: 'Ghaidan

and Lorna Abungu, *Lamu: Kenya's*
Enchanted Island (New York, Rizzoli
International Publications, 2009),
particularly at 66–67 with plates, and
78–79, 82–83, 69, 70, 71.
10 Personal communication, C. Orme-
Smith to authors, August 2006.

speculated that in Lamu, talismans were placed in the recessed niches that later held verses from the Quran or imported items such as the China plates.'[11]

In respect of Zanzibar of the period 1840 to 1860, Princess Emily Said-Ruete recorded that the niches displayed 'handsome cut glass, a plate beautifully painted, or an elegant tasteful jug. In addition, many homes featured ivory carvings and brass trays.'[12] Donley-Reid points out that during that period the same practice prevailed in western India, and cites the Bombay Gazeteer: 'At Ahmedabad in the houses of rich Sunni trading Bohoras the shelves are ornamented with rows of much-prized old china and spoons.'[13] This was true of other parts of Gujarat as well. Wilding notes examples in Surat and Rander.[14]

But fashions change over time, and so did both the design of the *zidaka*[15] and the nature of the displays in the recessed niches, as Romero rightly observes: 'Recently, and to illustrate change in fashions in home decorating styles, pictures of the patriarch of the family, or in some cases pictures of the entire family, are found on display in the niches.'[16]

When fine china and ceramics ceased to appear regularly, and then returned only intermittently, other items took their place, because the centuries-old house architecture, wall designs, and habits of display did not disappear. The Sultan's Palace in Stone Town, Zanzibar, a 19th century CE building, being a Muslim household, preserved the *zidaka*, although in their enlarged form, the *shubaka*.

Prof. Abdul Sheriff has pointed out the distinction between the *zidaka* and their larger counterpart in the Zanzibar Palace thus: 'The *vidaka* of the Swahili tradition were rather small and shallow finely carved plaster niches to hold single plates or items. The Zanzibar Palace represents the Omani architectural tradition that loses that craftsmanship; the walls are plain and there are large otherwise undecorated *shubaka* which could hold several plates or other large pieces. Both used the space to show off the owner's treasures, but somewhat differently.'[17]

In the Zanzibar Palace, these *shubaka* are incorporated into several public and private rooms. The State Room is a

---

11 Patricia W. Romero, *Lamu: History, Society and Family in an East African Port Society* (Princeton, Marcus Wiener, 1997), 40.
12 Emily Ruete (born Salme, Princess of Oman and Zanzibar), *Memoirs of an Arabian Princess from Zanzibar* (1886, Zanzibar, The Gallery, 1998 rev. translation), 20–23; Ghaidan, *Lamu* (Nairobi, EA Literature Bureau, 1976), 56.

13 *Bombay Gazeteer*, 'Gujarat Population: Mussalmans and Parsees', Vol. IX, 1899, in L. Donley-Reed (1984), 321–322.
14 Richard Wilding, 'The Ceramics of the Lamu Archipelago' (1977), PhD thesis, University of Nairobi, 557.
15 Ibid.
16 Patricia W. Romero, *Lamu: History, Society and Family in an East African Port Society* (Princeton, Marcus Wiener, 1997), 252.

17 Written communication from Prof. Abdul Sheriff, 30 August 2008.

notable example, with built-in *shubaka* on both sides of this long ceremonial room.

As the *zidaka* continued to be a part of late 19th century homes, the new pottery and ceramics from Europe (though visibly inferior, both artistically and in material, from their Chinese predecessors) began to fill these niches. Thus plates and bowls, principally from Holland and England, came to be placed in those niches. An illustration of this appears in Kiriama (2005).[18] Another such illustration, together with a discussion on the *zidaka*, may be seen in Middleton (1992).[19] Further, current use of Zanzibar plates in *zidaka* is shown in several illustrations in Abungu (2009).[20]

In palaces, the better of

18 Herman O. Kiriama, *The Swahili of the Kenya Coast* (Mombasa, Eight Publishers / National Museums of Kenya, 2005), 16.
19 John Middleton, *The World of the Swahili: An African Mercantile Civilization* (New Haven, Yale University Press, 1992).
20 George and Lorna Abungu, *Lamu: Kenya's Enchanted Island* (New York, Rizzoli International Publications, 2009).

the products from these later Western sources were used. English porcelain such as Crown Derby, Worcester Gilt, and Blue and White took the place of fine china. Examples of these can still be seen on the walls and in the niches in the Sultan's Palace (now the Palace Museum) in Zanzibar. Yet Maastricht and Maastricht-type ceramics also found their place alongside those finer pieces.

SUBSTITUTES IN COLLECTIONS

In addition to their place in the *zidaka*, cultured households had begun to adorn their walls and front rooms with collectibles in which fine china was prominent. During this period Sir John Kirk made drawings and took photographs of such displays.

'One of the illustrations by Sir John Kirk shows a wall covered by Chinese bowls in a private house.'[21]

By the end of the 19th century CE, collectors began to display Maastricht and Maastricht-type plates from Western Europe alongside Chinese ceramics acquired earlier or since. Thus in time such plates from Western Europe became decorative additions to or substitutes for fine china plates and bowls on walls and in *zidaka*. In collections, as in households, these new ceramics came to be added to the fine china already there.

A notable example of this was the collection of Seth Jaffer Dewji of the prominent

mercantile firm of Dewji Jamal and Company, which had been established in Zanzibar in the 1850s. Postcards published by *The Mombasa Times* in the mid-1920s show this well-known collection. Several Zanzibar plates can be seen among the Chinese vases and bowls, Persian carpets, and Yemeni arms. Seth Abdul Jaffer, Jaffer Dewji's son, is seated in the midst of them all (see illustrations and inset).[22]

The plates thus became both utilitarian in their use in the household and decorative in their presence in the front rooms.

---

21 Arthur E. Robinson, 'Notes on Saucer and Bowl Decorations on Houses, Mosques and Temples', in *Tanganyika Notes and Records* No. 10 (December 1940), 86 (7). This illustration was published in Brown, *The Story of Africa*.

22 From the turn of the century to the late 1920s, this collection was regularly visited by dignitaries and other visitors to the coast, including Mrs. Sarojini Naidu, Lord Kitchener, Winston Churchill, and Governor Sir Robert Coryndon. The collection was housed in the Jaffer Dewji family house in Government Square, opposite the Old Port entrance: *Daily Nation*, 23 March 1963; records of the family in the possession of his descendant, Mohamed Jaffer.

Two views of the Seth Jaffer Dewji Collection, with his son and fellow collector, Seth Abdul Jaffer, seated and inset. (Postcards from the Elchi Nowrojee Collection.)

THE MANUFACTURERS

THE MAIN manufacturers were in the Netherlands and England, with other significant producers in Germany. In the Netherlands, the principal manufacturers were Petrus Regout & Co. of Maastricht and the Société Céramique, also of Maastricht.

The firm of Petrus Regout & Co. was founded by Petrus Regout (1801–1878) in 1836. It introduced large-scale production of earthenware in mechanized factories using steam engines. After a slow start, when it had to compete with the already famous English earthenware on the market, the firm began prospering in the 1850s and then grew over the rest of the century to dominate the industry and to export its products all over the world.

Around 1869, the firm began to use its world-famous trademark of a sphinx couchant on a plinth. The company by then was also producing sanitary ware. In 1883 this logo was registered officially. In 1899 the company was renamed Sphinx.

The dating of the plates that carry the attribution 'Petrus Regout & Co.' with the logo of the sphinx can thus be put between 1869 and 1899. This constitutes almost all the plates from that source presently to be seen in the East African region, as it is rare to find one stamped and attributed with the word 'Sphinx'.

In 1891, Dutch manufacturers were obliged by law to stamp 'Made in Holland' for all exported items. This further narrows down the dating of such Petrus Regout items to the period 1891 to 1899.

Within these years, Petrus Regout & Co. used various marks to indicate the year of manufacture.

Another well-known manufacturer, the Société Céramique, originated in the factory firm founded in 1851 by Winand Clermont and Charles Chainaye, also in Maastricht. After a takeover by the Belgian engineer Guillaume Lambert in 1859 and other legal restructuring, the company emerged in 1863 as the Société Céramique. It flourished and over the following 40 years became the main competitor of Petrus Regout & Co.[1]

In the period after the First World War, the industry began to decline. Eventually, after the Second World War, Sphinx and Société Céramique merged in 1958 to become Sphinx Sanitair BV. By then, each had completed a century of production and together had produced almost 18,000 designs. In 1969, manufacture of earthenware pottery by the Maastricht companies came to an end after 133 years of production. Sphinx has since continued to manufacture sanitary ware and tiles to the present.

Among the German manufacturers, the most important was Villeroy & Bosch, a firm established in Wallerfangen in the Saar Basin in 1789 and still in active business all over the world. A prominent French manufacturer was Utzschneider & Co. of Sarrguemines, which had been established even earlier, in 1770. Their plates bore the mark 'Opaque de Sarreguemines'. Opaque refers to a type of porcelain. It was extremely popular in the Lamu market.

Prominent among the many British manufacturers were Worcester and Adams. Spode was another popular make in the Lamu market. Allen (1971) also mentions Lowestoft and Crown Derby.

THE PLATES

The early products of these manufacturers were cheap products for their local markets. Allen (1972) suggests that 'they were made for the peasant and petty-bourgeois market in France, Germany, Holland and Belgium but also occasionally for export to Eastern countries'. (See there also for illustration of three plates 'of the type most commonly used in Lamu houses'.) This market in Europe is reflected in the Dutch term for a plate collection, which is *Boerenbont*, as these items were 'mainly used by farmers, but the upper class and castle families took over their usage'.[2] A mid-nineteenth-century

1 For a fuller account of the history of the two firms, see A. Polling, *Maastrichtse Ceramiek* (Lochem, Untiek Uitgenersmaatschappy Antiek Lochem BV, 2001); also www. geheugenvannederland.nl and gvnnl/ handler.cfm. See also T. Volker, *Porcelain and the Dutch East India Company* (Leiden, 1971).

2 James de Vere Allen, *Lamu Town: A Guide* (Lamu, Allen, 1977). See also A. Polling, 'Boerenbont Aardewerk uit de Fabriek van Petrus Regout' (1988), *Antiek 23*, 267.

visitor to East Africa, Admiral M. Guillain, had already observed that 'all the crockery imported into the country [Zanzibar] is of very mediocre quality and priced accordingly.'[3]

THE CHINESE INFLUENCE AND COPIES

The Western European manufacturers found a very receptive market for their dishes, bowls, and storage jars. Their earliest forays into this overseas market dominated by the demand for Chinese ware logically commenced with copies of Chinese designs. Examples may be seen in the Fort Jesus Museum. These were inferior wares and poor copies. 'English Copy

of a Chinese Dish, Early 19th Century' in Fort Jesus, reproducing a peony pattern, confirms this view. As does the similar display in the National Museum in Dar es Salaam showing a 'fragment of a Dutch copy of a Chinese blue and white dish, with the original next to it'.

But the influence was much deeper than merely imitating patterns. Wilding sets it out: 'The debt owed by the European potters to their Chinese predecessors is immediately apparent. A glance at the sections of the Spode and Regout wares confirms this; a glance at the decorations emphasizes it. The extensive use of Chinese-inspired shapes, particularly of bowls and dishes, is a very notable feature of nineteenth century European ceramics.'[4]

To quote Kan Shuyi again: 'Imaginary visions of the East shaped European designs, resulting in landscapes, people, and animals that the Chinese and the Japanese would not have recognized... Chinese- and Japanese-style motifs appear on wares with European shapes...While the original inspiration may be in some sense Asian, the end results were often creative responses to local needs and tastes.'[5]

The most common imitations were of course replicas of the principal Chinese motifs, such as the willow pattern and other landscape designs.

Chinese blue and white continued to influence the manufacturers in Europe.

3 M. Guillain, *Documents sur l'Histoire, la Geographie et le Commerce de l'Afrique Orientale*, 3 Vols. (Paris, 1856–7) Vol. 3, 347, cited by Kirkman (1974).

4 Richard Wilding, 'The Ceramics of the

Lamu Archipelago' (1997), PhD thesis, University of Nairobi, 391.
5 Kan Shuyi, *Inspired By Japan and China: The Egawa Collection of European Ceramics* (Singapore, Asian Civilizations Museum, 2011), 19.

Many later plates still used the distinctive blue, in darker or lighter shades, for designs quite different from the Chinese models. An example can be seen in the Beit-el-Ajaib Museum, Zanzibar. In another variant, Chinese patterns were continued, but the blue was dropped and new colours were used, so that, for example, we can find willow pattern plates from Holland in pink or in pale green.

PEASANT FLORAL

Original designs, of course, did come to take the place of these copies. Several considerations affected the choice of these designs. Among them were Western Europe's own concepts of what would appeal to markets in diverse countries, and the Indian Ocean countries were major markets.

Floral designs in numerous variations were the principal offerings. These later settled into repeated patterns. The dominant colours were purples, mauves, and greens in combinations of dark and pale, lines and curves. Flowers, moons, leaves, and tendrils embellish the plates.

Wilding, starting with L. R. Whiter's description of this as 'peasant-style painting', uses the term 'Peasant Floral' as a generic description of the style, and the products as 'European Peasant Floral Ware',[6] recalling the humble origins Allen (1972) had mentioned (see above).

There is no delicacy in this heavy stoneware, and no pretence at finesse in the designs. This is not the work of master potters. This is factory-made ware. This was transfer-printed earthenware. It allowed standardization and mass production, although there were also hand-painted products. The painters make no claim to fine art, and most

designs and the handwork are broad strokes and unsubtle though pleasing patterns. They are not the restricted produce for palace or connoisseur, but mass-produced wares for a market being aggressively expanded.

There were occasional departures from this approach and the usual market. The Ghalia Collection holds examples of these as well. These are large and exceptionally fine plates in translucent colours. These are obviously not tableware, nor are they for domestic purposes. They are decorative and display items.

GOLD-LEAF WARE

Another exception to the usual products was Dutch ware with patterns in gold-leaf instead of paint. Examples of this are a bowl and a plate (illustrations). They are white with gold on the rims, the cusp, and the base. Around the body of the bowl where the

6 Richard Wilding, 'The Ceramics of the Lamu Archipelago' (1977), PhD thesis, University of Nairobi, 398.

51

usual floral patterns of green and purple paint would be is a similar floral pattern, but of embedded gold-leaf.

The floral pattern is stylized and regular, contrasting with the usual freer renderings of the design and brush strokes that mark the painted flowers and leaves.

The items were manufactured by the Société Céramique, indicating that they were manufactured after 1863. On the base is printed 'Societe Ceramique Maestricht. Made in Holland'. The latter words indicate that the bowls were made after 1891. The bowls have been acquired from south India. On the glaze is engraved writing which denotes the household they belonged to. This confirms that, apart from their intrinsic value, they were treated as silverware was

treated, engraved with the family's initials and passed on as heirlooms.

It may also be noticed that while plates and bowls with gold leaf may occasionally be found, cups and saucers are much less so and are now, even for the usual designs, much rarer in collections or antique shops.

THE ISLAMIC INFLUENCE

The Western manufacturers and their designers in time came to appreciate that an overwhelming part of the Indian Ocean market lay in lands which were largely Muslim or Muslim ruled, from Indonesia to the Gulf countries to Zanzibar. This is also borne out by Sadiq Ghalia's observation that the Ghalia Collection has been gathered almost exclusively from

countries with large Muslim markets—Zanzibar, Kenya, India, Tanzania, Indonesia, Bangladesh, and Yemen.

Accordingly, the crescent and star appear in many designs. An example of these is a green bowl carrying the crescent and star on the rim outside and also on the inside bottom of the bowl.

Wilding considered that these designs were occasional. He wrote, 'Just occasionally, peasant floral designs occur which were made specifically for the Middle Eastern market. One popular modification for the orient is a white moon and star on a red field, either as a body reserve, or as a centre badge.'[7]

With the benefit of greater comparative material and the spread of a major collection (the Ghalia Collection), this

---

7 Ibid.

view may respectfully be corrected. The crescent and star design was not produced 'just occasionally', but was a prominent design for a prominent market (see illustrations, page 15). It was regularly used with the basic Peasant Floral patterns. Its eminence was also emphasized by its use in the more prestigious calligraphic designs that followed.

The crescent and star appeared usually on green plates, but also unusually, and with striking effect, on blue plates and deep terracotta-coloured plates, as may be seen in the Ghalia Collection.

The widespread examples are of the usual floral design with the crescent and star added on the bottom of the dish. An attractive example can be seen in the Beit-el-Ajaib Museum, Zanzibar.

In compliance with the expectations of that market, no human faces or figures appear as designs on these plates. Floral patterns dominate overwhelmingly. But plates

also had calligraphic and, later, geometric designs, both well within the Islamic tradition.

Animals too are absent. Unusually, two examples have been seen. One (illustration) shows a cockerel repeated on the quarters inside the plate. The other is in the Lamu Museum and depicts an elephant with its mahout astride.[8] This is clearly for the Indian market, but these are rarities and in the large Ghalia Collection itself there is no representation of any animal.

Calligraphic Designs
Though not very common, calligraphic designs were a significant part of the genre. These were plates with the calligraphy incorporated into traditional designs or itself dominating the design. The calligraphy could be:
A) of a religious nature
B) of a commercial nature
C) for a state purpose
D) for a purely decorative purpose

8 Reproduced in ibid., Plate 267/2.

لا اله الا الله
یا ابو بکر
یا عمر
الله وحده لا شريك له
محمد رسول الله
یا عثمان
یا علی
لا اله الا الله

56

Excellent examples of the first three can be seen in the Beit-el-Ajaib Museum, Zanzibar, and in the Ghalia Collection.

Calligraphy of a Religious Nature

In the first category (A), the plate displayed in the Beit-el-Ajaib Museum has a simple, broad floral border with a wide shallow base on which is an Islamic inscription. Both the border pattern and the calligraphy are in light blue upon the plain white ceramic of the plate.

The plate itself is of English (not Dutch) manufacture. It does not carry the manufacturer's name, but on the verso it carries an identifiable diamond-shaped mark.

S. W. Fisher explains: 'A diamond-shaped mark, printed or impressed, is often seen on wares first made between 1842 and 1883, indicating that to prevent piracy, the particular design had been

registered with the London Patent Office. It will of course be clear that the information thus given in the marks will only indicate the earliest possible date of manufacture, since the design so registered could have been continued in succeeding years.'[9] The letters and numbers on the diamond mark show the class of the item (for registration purposes); the parcel number; the year, month, and day of its first manufacture; and the

9 S. W. Fisher, *English Pottery and Porcelain Marks* (Slough, W. Foulsham, 1970).

initials R or RD to indicate registration.

The marks (see illustration) in the diamond on the plate decipher, in accordance with lists set out in Fisher, as 'IV' = Class IV, 'Y' = 1853, 'I' = July, '4' = Fourth, '2' = Parcel No. 2. Thus the earliest date of manufacture of that particular design was 4 July 1853.

This was before the establishment of the seat of the Sultanate in the islands themselves (in 1856). Thus it is possible that this was an import into Oman brought to Zanzibar. More likely, it was the use of an earlier 1853 design that was stamped on the plates then imported subsequently directly into Zanzibar.

A major stream of Quranic calligraphy on these plates embodied the names of the first disciples of the Prophet (Peace Be Upon Him) and the names of the principal angels. These are found with the usual floral patterns embellishing the script, but also with the script alone. A very fine example of the latter from Petrus Regout is illustrated. On a plain white background, with no other design or colour, the names of the archangels and the disciples alternate. Jibreel, Ali (the Fourth Caliph), Israfeel, Uthmaan (the Third Caliph), Izraeel, Umar (the Second Caliph), Mikaeel, and Abu Bakr (the First Caliph) radiate out from the words in a circle in the centre: Mohamed Nabi-ul-Rehman. The words are in a cursive script.

Another plate (Société Céramique) in the same collection has similar votary calligraphy, but in a completely different setting. With a blue floral border, the large centre has three lines also in a cursive script in dark blue on a white background: *Allahu wahdahu laa sharika lahu, Mohamed Rasulullah. Fainnaka mansurra.* (There is no God but Allah. He has no associates or partner. Mohamed is the Prophet

of Allah. Assuredly you are victorious.)

These plates follow a very old tradition in Islamic art. By the ninth century, calligraphy had appeared on ceramics. A beautiful example of this is a white earthenware bowl in the Museum of Islamic Arts in Doha, Qatar, with an inscription in an ornamental Kufic script.[10]

In the following century, calligraphy also appeared on Persian ceramics from Nishapur in the Khurassan and from Samarkand in Central Asia, all these being among the earliest use of Arabic text as surface decoration.[11] A particularly fine example of these bowls and plates is in the Freer Gallery

of Art in Washington, DC, also with exquisite Kufic script bordering and embellishing the centre of a large plate.[12]

Outstanding examples of Quranic calligraphy are in the Ghalia Collection. Among these are some very large Maastricht plates now rarely found. Some of these are 70 centimetres (36 inches) across. They are of exceedingly fine colours—deep translucent reds, blues, and greens.

*

Calligraphy is a key form of Islamic art.[13] It carries the

10 Alexandria Gouveia, 'A Cultured Pearl', *Oryx*, November 2008, 64–70. See also S. Flury, 'Ornamental Kufic Inscriptions on Pottery' in J. A. Pope (ed.), *A Survey of Persian Art* (London, 1939), 1643.
11 Ernest J. Grube, *The World of Islam* (London, Paul Hamlyn, 1966), 45–46. See also Charles K. Wilkinson, *Nishapur: Pottery of the Early Islamic Period* (New York, Metropolitan Museum of Art, n.d.) and David Talbot Rice, *Islamic Art* (London, Thames & Hudson, 1965, 1975).

12 The emergence of the Kufic script and its variations during the eighth century and its gradual decline in the Middle East during the tenth (as more cursive scripts came into use and were reformed into 'the proportioned scripts' under the direction of Ibn Muqla and the geometric principles laid down by him) help to date these ceramics. See David J. Roxburgh, *Writing the Word of God: Calligraphy and the Qur'an* (Houston, Museum of Fine Arts, 2007).
13 Calligraphy has been, through the centuries, a constant part of Islamic architectural decorative design, paintings, ceramics, tiles, book illuminations, the enhancements of mosques, documents of state including *tughras* (examples are of the Ottoman Emperors, and nearer home, of the Sultans of Zanzibar), textiles, glass, and

illumination of the language of the Revelation.

Its instrument, the Pen, is of special importance. Scholars have stated that 'the symbol of a permanent revelation is the mystic Pen and the mystic Record'.

The Pen is a prominent part of the first revelation: see Surah 96 verse 4 ('He who taught [the use of] the Pen taught man what he knew not'). And as well of the second revelation: see Surah

68 verse 1 ('By the Pen and by the Record which men write...'). Indeed, the very title of Surah 68 is The Pen.

But in these Surahs, 'Pen' is much more than an instrument of writing. It has comprehensive meanings. Within the harmony of these many meanings, the word encompasses 'reading, writing, books, study, knowledge, research', bringing all forms of the creativity of the mind to the faithful.

The Quranic calligraphy on the plates thus resonated differently to different users, and differently in their different uses.

Calligraphy for Commercial Purposes

In respect of calligraphy for commercial purposes (B above), the Beit-el-Ajaib Museum, Zanzibar, displays a fine example.

The plate displayed has a typical floral design in the familiar colours—purple,

ivories. See for example Yasin Hamid Safadi, *Islamic Calligraphy* (London, Thames & Hudson, 1978/1987); Oliver Watson, *Ceramics from Islamic Lands* (New York/Kuwait, Thames & Hudson/ Kuwait National Museum, 2004); Dr. Rehana Raja, *Masjid Sheikh Muhammed Bashir & Runda Islamic Centre* (Nairobi, As Zahra Foundation, 2015); the exhibition *Sultan Ali of Mashad, Master of Nastaliq* at the Metropolitan Museum of Art, New York, April 2001–April 2002; Hamo Sassoon, *Siwas of Lamu* (Nairobi, Lamu Society, 1975) and the exquisite carved Siwa from Lamu at the Nairobi National Museum; and the permanent exhibits of ceramics at the Fort Jesus Museum, Mombasa. Like the Sheikh Muhammud Bashir Mosque at Runda (2015), the new Ithna Asheri Mosque in Mombasa has prominent calligraphy, both on the outside and the inside of the mosque. Fort Jesus Museum, Mombasa, has also featured calligraphy in the newly (2017) restored Mazrui Hall in the fort.

blue, and pale green—and the familiar design of leaves and clove buds, but with a distinctive difference: in the centre there is an inscription in Arabic, surrounded by oak leaves. The inscription reads: 'Fuzoud Brothers and Company.' The inscription and its immediate border are pale grey in colour.

On the verso are two marks. Impressed into the clay are the words 'Made in England'. Printed under the glaze is a shield and crown, with 'F. B. & Co.' across the blazon, and below the shield the words 'Peera Dewjee Zanzibar'.

'F. B. & Co.' denotes Frank Beardmore & Co., the makers of the plate. Peera Dewji (Dewjee) was one of the most prominent of manufacturer's agents in Zanzibar. His name appears on many other plates. Another example is in Fort Jesus Museum on a lustre ware bowl found, and now exhibited, there. The importance

of such agents is dealt with below.

Incised under the glaze are the words 'Made in England'. Fisher (1970) states that the presence of these words 'signifies a 20th century origin.' That is borne out by the fact that Beardmore's period of operations was 1903 to 1914.[14]

Fuzoud Brothers and Company had also commissioned a similarly inscribed plate in other colours and a different design.

A plate marked with such calligraphy would have been in use in the business of the commissioning customer.

Another instance of plates commissioned for commercial promotional purposes may be seen in the National Museum in Dar es Salaam. Displayed there is a middle-sized bowl with a typical Maastricht-type purple-and-green floral design. The bottom has printed on it the form of a standing lion together with the words

14 James Kirkman, *Fort Jesus* (Oxford, The Clarendon Press, 1974), 123.

'Deutsch Ost Afrikanische Gessellschaft', the whole in a black circle. The DOAG was the German East Africa Company.

A plate produced for the DOAG is also illustrated by Aldrick. As with the bowl above, the company's name does not appear in any calligraphic form on the front of the plate, but is stamped on the reverse together with its seal.[15]

Calligraphy for a State Purpose

An example of the use of calligraphy for a state purpose, C above, may be seen in the Beit-el-Ajaib Museum, Zanzibar. It is a large handsome plate. The design is in a deep blue upon a plain white background. The broad border has a circular vine of berries doubled in a mirror image. Smaller concentric circles of simpler borders and rosettes

lead into the centre of the plate where there is an inscription in Arabic in green letters, surrounded by a thin ring of oak leaves. It reads *Dawlat al-Zanjibar* (Kiswahili: *Dola ya Zanzibar*; English: Wealth of Zanzibar).

The inscription and its border are also reproduced on its verso, also in colour, together with the printed mark of the manufacturer. This is a shield with a crown and the mark of its French manufacturer, Opaque de Sarrguemines. The calligraphy marks the plate, and presumably other similar items, as state property.

A similar plate, but without the floral border on the verso, may also be seen.

These types of texts are to be distinguished from the coats of arms on the dinner services in the use of successive Sultans (which are displayed separately in the museum). However, the plate on display is translucent and much finer than the Sultan's dinner plates,

and than the usual Maastricht-type plates, though not as fine as old china.

Examples of the individual dinner services in use in the reigns of Sultan Sayyid Bargash (1870–1888), Sultan Sayyid Hamed bin Thuwan (1893–1896), and Sultan Sayyid Khalifa bin Harub (1911–1960), bearing their coats of arms, can be seen in the Beit-el-Ajaib Museum, Zanzibar, the Palace Museum, Zanzibar, and the Fort Jesus Museum, Mombasa.

Calligraphy for Decorative Purposes

Secular calligraphic inscriptions are also present (D above). A fine example of such an inscription (though one that still invokes religious blessings) is a very attractive bowl on exhibition in the Fort Jesus Museum, Mombasa. This major piece is a wedding bowl with Arabic text in purple and gold leaf in five floral groups within the bowl, which is

15 Judith Aldrick, 'The Painted Plates of Zanzibar' (1997), *29 Kenya Past and Present*, 26.

otherwise all white, save for the rim, which mirrors the colours of the text. The text reads: 'Praise God and thou wilt attain joy and health, sweetness in drinking and the quenching of thirst; drink from the clear spirit of the Hassans, which will be a cure for every ill.'

Of French manufacture, this beautiful piece was acquired in Mombasa in the 1930s by Mrs. J. C. White, a benefactor of the Fort Jesus Museum, whose collection was one of those that formed the basis of the Fort Jesus collections when the museum opened in 1960.

In respect of such and other more mundane inscriptions, it is well to keep in mind Oliver Watson's caution that 'many "inscriptions" on pottery are purely decorative, and that an exact rendering was probably never intended and is probably not possible; not all inscriptions are meaningful.'[16]

They do not always merit undue scrutiny. Many inscriptions became standard additions.

GEOMETRIC PATTERNS

Geometric patterns followed later. Usually, these were Indonesian designs. Wilding comments on this: 'Equally extraordinary is the effort put in by both the Société Céramique and Petrus Regout at Maastricht to reproduce Indonesian patterns. These were executed in lustre printing and were very popular in the Lamu Archipelago.'[17]

CLOVE PATTERNS

Zanzibar itself also contributed to design patterns. Zanzibar's importance as a market was reflected in the frequent use of the clove motif. This was often stylized into a circular rosette pattern.[18] The clove pattern was of interest not only to Zanzibar. Indonesia, also a producer of cloves and simultaneously a large buyer of Zanzibari cloves, itself having introduced the crop to Zanzibar,[19] was another principal market for these earthenware plates and shared enthusiasm for the design.

16 Oliver Watson, *Ceramics From Islamic Lands: The Al-Sabah Collection, Kuwait National Museum* (New York, Thames & Hudson / Kuwait National Museum, 2005), 91.
17 Richard Wilding, 'The Ceramics of the Lamu Archipelago' (1977), PhD thesis, University of Nairobi, 396.
18 Judith Aldrick, 'The Painted Plates of Zanzibar' (1997), *29 Kenya Past and Present*, 26.
19 Abdul Sheriff, *Slaves, Spices and Ivory in Zanzibar* (London, James Currey, 1987).

THE MANUFACTURERS' AGENTS

ANOTHER SOURCE OF designs emerged from the marketing infrastructure that 19th century manufacturers in Europe set up around the world, reflecting the development of commerce on the global scale that Pannikar talks of. This relied heavily on the appointment of Commission Agents in major ports in every country, servicing through them the hinterland too.

The chain of agencies did not arise just out of business efficiency (though it was a supremely efficient system). It was fuelled by the desire to dominate markets through the establishment of distributive monopolies in different regions, areas, or towns, effected through these exclusive agencies in specific regions, and more particularly in the markets all over the globe.

On the aspect of design, agents were relied upon not only to determine the size of the market and therefore of the orders, but also to discern and convey the design preferences of customers in those markets. The factory sent out its own representatives to markets abroad, who would stop off at the principal ports on the routes of established shipping lines (such as P&O, the Deutsch Ost-Afrika Linie, the Union-Castle, and the British-India Steam Navigation Company). At each port, these factory representatives met with their agents, reviewed the market, discussed old and

new designs, and took orders. The appointed country agents were thus important players in the development of the market and of new designs. The export distribution structures of German postcard manufacturers, who also were busy in Deutsche Ost Afrika and Zanzibar between 1898 and 1914, are a model (see also Woody 1998).

The template may also be seen at work in the *kanga* (*khanga*, *leso*) business during this period, with the input of the local agent visible in the development of the product. As in respect of the plates, and during the same period, the famous Mombasa agent Kaderina Hajee Essak (whose firm had been established in 1887) played a major role in the shaping of the product. This manifested itself firstly in the enlargement of the unit size (from handkerchief to the size we know today), and secondly in the incorporation of the Swahili motto at the insistence of Kaderina Hajee Essak.[1]

The importance of the local agent or Commission Agent in the Zanzibar plates trade was often acknowledged by the factory. This was done by printing the agent's name as part of the manufacturing details on the base of the wares. A number of the Zanzibar agents were so acknowledged.

Examples are: Peera Dewji, Sumar Hassum, and Abdool Hoosein Bros. & Co.

Kirkman states that 'Peera Dewji was a Customs Master of Zanzibar who retired and set up an importing business'.[2] Peera Dewji is recalled in the memoirs of Princess Salme, the daughter of Sultan Sayyid Said (1806–1856), while speaking of her visit to Zanzibar in 1885 during the reign of Sultan Bargash. It is in unflattering terms: 'This Pera Daudji [sic], a very wily and cunning Hindoo, has become the Sultan's jack-of-all-trades. The lamp-cleaner of old now devotes his services to the sovereign of Zanzibar in the highest and lowest positions. All diplomatic negotiations pass through his hands, but the same hands wait upon the

---

1 Tony Troughear, 'Khangas, Bangles and Baskets' (1983), *Kenya Past and Present* No. 16, 11, 13. For examples, see Javed Jafferji and Nadin Hadi, *Kanga Wisdom: A Collection of Kanga Sayings* (Zanzibar, Gallery Publications, 2007); Jeanette Hanby and David Bygott, *Kanga: 101 Uses* (Nairobi, Haria's Stamps, 1984/2008), 12; Christel de Wit and Zarina Patel, 'Language of the Kanga', *Awaaz* Issue II (2004), 55, 56; Khadija Abu, 'The Significant Role of the Kanga Cloth in East Africa' (2001), BA thesis, Buckinghamshire Chilterns University College; John Vanco and Kelly Armour, *Kanga: Wrap Garments from East Africa* (Erie, PA, Erie Art Museum, 2008).

2 James Kirkman, *Fort Jesus* (Oxford, The Clarendon Press, 1974), 122.

guests of the Sultan's table. His salary, thirty dollars a month, every one will admit to be a low one, but I was told that he made it worth anyone's while to increase it. This omnipotent Pera Daudji is not above bartering his influence...The court jeweller who refused to give a certain percentage on all orders to the ex-lamp-cleaner, lost his custom in consequence. Pera Daudji honoured and entrusted a more accommodating competitor with the execution of such orders.'[3]

Dewji was, however, a trusted officer of the Sultan and additionally managed Bargash's fleet of steamships. After his retirement from government service, he became, as mentioned earlier, an agent, including for Frank Beardmore & Co. The dates of operation of this manufacturer, 1903 to 1914,[4] date also

a part at least of the period of Peera Dewji's agency and business operations.

Aldrick gives details of Abdool Hoossein Bros. & Co., a firm opened in Zanzibar in 1869 and in Mombasa in 1896.[5]

The two names, however, are of the same family interests, because the firm of Abdool Hoossein Bros. & Co. was founded by Peera Dewji himself.[6] Playne and Gale give greater detail and in a laudatory vein, in sharp contrast to the Princess:

'Born in 1841, [Peera Dewji] entered the service of the Sultan Bhargash at an early age. He was held in high esteem by that ruler, for his zeal and honesty. He accompanied His Highness on his famous visit to India and at a later date paid a similar visit to England...In 1903 he

3 Emily Ruete (born Salme, Princess of Oman and Zanzibar), *Memoirs of an Arabian Princess from Zanzibar*, (Zanzibar, The Gallery, 1886, 1998 revised translation), 202.
4 James Kirkman, *Fort Jesus* (Oxford, The Clarendon Press, 1974), 123.

5 Judith Aldrick, 'The Painted Plates of Zanzibar' (1997), 29, *Kenya Past and Present* 27.
6 S. Playne and F. Gayle, *East Africa (British)* (London, Foreign and Colonial Compiling and Publishing Company, 1909), 419.

was once more in London to attend the Coronation of King Edward VII....'[7]

Aldrick's 2015 biography of Peera Dewji, *The Sultan's Spymaster*, gives a fully detailed and more rounded view of his many-sided public activities.[8]

Aldrick (1997) also records a plate that is marked on the reverse 'Petrus Regout & Co., Maastricht', which words she states are 'over-stamped in Gujerati' with the name of the agent. The agent from India, whose name is not given, 'liked his name over-stamped in Gujerati, and it seems that these plates were imported undecorated into India, where they were painted and glazed before the trader exported them to East Africa.'[9] The design of this plate incorporates lotus flowers, and Aldrick considers that 'the design has

a distinctly Indian flavour and was painted in India'.[10]

Ghalia notes that, on the thousands of plates he has seen and on those in his collection, the only agents whose names feature on the plates are those from Zanzibar, even though his collection has numerous plates from Indonesia, India, and Yemen. This says much about the influence of the Zanzibari agents with the manufacturers. It also speaks about the extent of their markets and thus about their entrepreneurial abilities and energy. The Zanzibari agents held a pre-eminent place in the eyes of the Dutch and English manufacturers of the plates.

This was a consequence of the significant increase in the volume of sales over the years. Wilding explains, 'In the last quarter of the nineteenth century, the market was sufficiently great for agents in Zanzibar, and less often in Mombasa and Dar-es-Salaam,

7 Ibid.
8 Judy Aldrick, *The Sultan's Spymaster: Peera Dewji of Zanzibar* (Naivasha, Old Africa Books, 2015).
9 Judith Aldrick, 'The Painted Plates of Zanzibar' (1997), 29, *Kenya Past and Present* 27.

10 Ibid. 28.

to order in bulk and apply their own stamp.'[11]

Wilding himself also illustrates some of the marks of the East African agents.[12] Of interest are a mark of Peera Dewji's company, Abdool Hoossein Bros. & Co., of a design other than their usual belt. Plates with this third mark were thus also his imports.

Wilding also illustrated a mark of 'Jern. Lyon & Co., Zanzibar'. Another mark that he records, of Amritlal & Company of Nairobi, shows that the agency is of the post-1921 period, and therefore of much later manufactures.

The situation regarding acknowledgement of the agent's name is also reflected in the *kanga* trade. There also

the name of the Mombasa agent, Kaderina Hajee Essak, was often acknowledged by being printed on the product. His name and the words *'Mali ya Abdulla'* featured from the time of the early *kangas*.[13] This imprint remains till the present.

The plates also evidence that this was a large Anglophone market and was distinct from that in the Dutch East Indies and other Dutch colonies. The stamped or incised colophons on the reverse of the plates use English to indicate the country of manufacture ('Made in Holland'). Even though the Dutch East Indies was a captive market for Maastricht, the use of English indicates that there was another major

market on this western side of the Indian Ocean that it was profitable to address directly. Ghalia has found no names of agents on the plates he has acquired from the former Dutch East Indies markets, and we should assume that the Maastricht factories had their own representatives in Batavia city. (Evidence that the Dutch East Indies were always a major market is reflected in the use by Petrus Regout of designs that he marketed under names such as 'Bali'.)

11 Richard Wilding, 'The Ceramics of the Lamu Archipelago' (1977), PhD thesis, University of Nairobi, 399.
12 Ibid. Plate 258 (25–29).

13 Jeanette Hanby and David Bygott, *Kanga: 101 Uses* (1984; Nairobi, Haria's Stamps, 2008), 12.

LATER MANUFACTURERS AND PRESENT TRENDS

THE SUCCESS OF this earthenware came eventually, in ironic fashion, to generate imitators of its own, just as a hundred years earlier it had itself imitated its Chinese rivals.[1] Manufacturers in Japan and elsewhere put copies and competing products on the market. From Japan came plates from Ideal Iron Stone Ware and S.S. Crown producing Sasai Iron Stone China. Mass production of crockery and changing tastes were however already signalling the end.

Zanzibar plates began to fade away from the market after the end of the First World War. Notwithstanding this, as late as the post-war 1940s, such earthenware came out of occupied Japan, stepping in for the devastated factories in war-ravaged Europe. But such production was only an Indian summer.

Later, sporadically, plates came on the scene to commemorate various public events. Examples are those produced in the early 1960s to celebrate 'Uhuru Tanganyika' and 'Jamhuri Tanganyika' (Shaila Mauladad-Fisher and David Fisher Collection). These 1961 and 1962 plates

Villoo Nowrojee Collection

---

1 There were earlier imitations. Oliver Watson, *Ceramics From Islamic Lands: The Al-Sabah Collection*, Kuwait National Museum (New York, Thames & Hudson / Kuwait National Museum, 2005), 33, notes that 'rather undistinguished porcelain in the European style was made briefly in Istanbul towards the end of the 19th century', citing Arthur Lane, *Later Islamic Pottery: Persia, Syria, Egypt, Turkey* (London, 1957; 2nd Edition 1971), 66.

do not pretend to any artistic merit, but do reflect that older social habits about decorating homes with Zanzibar plates were still extant, as they are today, and that exceptional contemporary events of a national nature, as opposed to personal religious devotion, also came to influence these products.

These late items were not the plates of any of the major producers of the past. As the faulty spelling on the plate with the flag shows (see illustration), these were brought on the market by less organized producers. The persons involved in the production of these plates were not familiar with either the event they were commemorating or its geography. It is more likely these were items donated for the October 1961 Tanganyika Independence celebrations than objects put up for general sale in the market. However, the flag on the one plate

(which is the Tanganyika African National Union flag and not the national flag to be) is vividly drawn and coloured. It is a pleasant coda for the genre.

Though production and sales came to an end early in the 20th century, large numbers of the earlier Maastricht plates fortunately remained in use in numerous households for the next 50 years.

They also remained available, though not necessarily in shops. During the period 1905 to 1925, it was a common sight for Zanzibar plates to be sold on the roadside in Mombasa (see illustrations).

*

In the succeeding 50 years to the present, Zanzibar plates and *zidaka* have remained favoured interior decoration. Javed Jafferji and Elie Losleben record several attractive examples of hotels and private

houses from Lamu, Zanzibar, and Mombasa using this decor.[2]

But occasionally we can also see the use of the Zanzibari plate on the exterior of a house. Again, the question of its purpose there arises, and suggests that old beliefs may not after all have been wholly given up. A recent example can be seen on a modern business building in the Malindi seafront area. P. K. Building, a 1970s construction, has embedded on its concrete frontage two blue-and-white willow/floral pattern plates.

Happily, all this disparate, and often even ill-intentioned, historical mix nonetheless has resulted in a large number of appealing objects. Though they could not compete with the marvels of Chinese pottery and ceramics, they eventually came to be a pleasing oeuvre of their own. It is one that

2 Javed Jafferji and Elie Losleben, *Swahili Style* (Zanzibar, Gallery Publications, 2005).

Earthen Pots at a Native selling Place. Mombasa B. E. A.

Postcards from the Elchi Nowrojee Collection

545.   A STREET WENDER, MOMBASA.

in the recent past has been increasingly appreciated and collected, examples of which we can fortunately still acquire and enjoy. The enlargement of this appreciation has led to an increase in the number of collectors, and in Ghalia's view this is a good thing, leading as it has to the better preservation of these plates.

THE GHALIA COLLECTION

The leading collection of these plates, covering East Africa and the Indian Ocean, is that of the late Sadiq Ghalia of Mombasa. Comprising over 3,500 items, this attractive and comprehensive collection affords scholars an unrivalled base for an authoritative study and consideration of the subject in our context. These objects offer us much

of our past and much material to unravel it. Our material culture must not remain unexamined. A major part of our understanding of our region and ourselves in it comes from our understanding of our art treasures. Such art, common also to others, makes us therefore more aware of our shared history and our realization that we are not just a decades-old 'nation' but also a component of older and larger historical units, and that that history is a major part of the Kenyan heritage. Kenya does not have only a Bantu heritage. It has a Cushitic heritage, a Nilotic heritage, a Hamitic heritage, a British heritage, and an old and very manifest Indian Ocean heritage, tying us with the islands to the south, and in the north and east with the Horn, Arabia,

the Gulf, Iran, the Indian Subcontinent, and Indonesia in the arc of the littoral.

This is seen in the items and in the sources of the Ghalia Collection. As mentioned earlier, the items were acquired in Zanzibar, Mombasa, Indonesia, Bangladesh, Yemen, and India, reminding us of those shared cultures and shared pasts. These sources also confirm the spread of these wares in their business prime. The Ghalia Collection is a major reference point in the region to use for comparative studies in several fields, including the history of art and international trade.

This heritage is also seen in our national museums. In speaking of the items in the Fort Jesus Museum, James Kirkman writes, 'The whole collection illustrates

the cosmopolitan culture which the Coast has enjoyed for centuries. Except for the local earthenware, all items of collection found on the Coast could have been found on the coasts of South Arabia, Persia, India and Ceylon.'[3]

The Ghalia Collection has been a process spread over the past 50 years and thus gives a valuable representative spread of both use and retention over a long period in several countries.

Another important collection is the Orme-Smith Collection of Chris and Teresa Orme-Smith. This consists of two parts. One is a large number of Chinese vases, glazed and unglazed. These were given to the National Museums of Kenya and are on display in the Large Museum at Gedi. The other part is a collection of about 400 plates, bowls, and dishes.[4] These are predominantly from the Maastricht producers, but also from a number of English and German factories, with a lesser number of later Japanese products.

It is also important to look at items in the homes of coast families. These emphasize the old usage and continuity of these items in households in Mombasa, Zanzibar, Malindi, and Lamu. Some of these plates have been in the same family and in use for well over 100 years. The handing down within families of old china is not at all unusual.

An example of fine china passed on in a family was recorded in 1936: 'The bowl illustrated was given to the writer by the late Kadhi of Mafia, Ali bin Athman, a few months before his death in March 1935. The donor stated that the bowl had been in his family for three hundred years. According to ceramic experts

---

3 James Kirkman, 'Fort Jesus Museum Collection', *Kenya Past and Present*, Vol. 1, No. 2 (April 1972), 9.

4 Personal communication to the authors, 15 June 2004, and other correspondence.

in London, it is a fourteenth century Ming period trade piece.'[5]

Another such example was 'the precious china bowl of the Mwenyi Mkuu, the designation of the former indigenous rulers of Zanzibar, out of which, according to tradition, they ate their rice for 40 years, and which Mr. Oscar Raphael at the time pronounced to be 350 years old. This bowl possesses great sentimental interest for the natives of Zanzibar.'[6]

The rarer plates with Quranic calligraphy were often reserved for use at home in religious ceremonies. Thus, like the earlier use of fine Chinaware, Zanzibar plates too came to be used for religious purposes as for secular purposes, in homes as in mosques. That they were used carefully and kept with care may be gauged from the remarkably good condition of so many of these plates, even though many are well over 100 years old. Some plates

found in shops are pocked, the glaze and pattern eaten away in places. It is likely that they were part of items hidden away in difficult times by being buried, and the glaze was unable to withstand the chemicals in the soil.[7] They started out as objects of utility, became part of the social and cultural practices of the communities, and are now *objets d'art*.

It is therefore important to submit these objects to more systematic study and critical examination, and to increase access of these most pleasurable objects to a wider

---

5 T. M. Revington, 'Note on the Bowl Mentioned on Page 36 of Tanganyika Notes and Records No. 1 of March 1936', *Tanganyika Notes and Records* No. 2 (October 1936), 110.
6 R. H. Crofton, *Zanzibar Affairs 1914– 1933* (London, Francis Edwards, 1953),

49–50. This bowl was acquired in 1925 for the Peace Museum, Zanzibar, from Lady Cave from a handsome donation made by Mr. Rudolph Said-Ruete, the son of Princess Sayyida Salme, Emily Ruete.

7 Fort Jesus Museum note.

audience and to keep enlarging that audience. Presently, there is need to document[8] systematically this area of the social and cultural history of our region, and by doing so to emphasize our regional context and the areas of shared histories, in particular among Zanzibar-Pemba, Lamu, the Tanzania coast and mainland, and the Kenya coast and mainland.

---

8 Examples of Zanzibar plates may be seen in all our museums and in numerous private households and collections. There are examples in Fort Jesus Museum (Mombasa), Beit-el-Ajaib Museum (Zanzibar), the Palace Museum (Zanzibar), the National Museum and House of Culture (Dar es Salaam), Lamu Museum (Lamu), the National Museum (Nairobi, the Lamu Room), Malindi Museum (Malindi), and Kenya National Archives (Nairobi, with an example from the Murumbi Collection set in a typical *kidaka*). Though many of these are fine examples, displays need to increase to significant numbers and be sufficiently representative.

CONCLUSION

THE DUTCH DESIGNERS and Maastricht ware were latecomers in responding to the markets of Islamic rulers and lands. Chinaware had reacted much earlier.

Changes in style had been made as early as in the 14th century CE by certain producers in south China. After commenting on these, Watson states, 'There is an accumulation of evidence that points to this new ware being made specifically in a perceived Islamic style, and intended initially for export to the Middle East.'[1]

This was then followed in the early 17th century CE by Chinese kilns and designers incorporating Quranic and other sayings in Arabic into their products for these markets. Occasionally reference was also made to specific patrons such as the Moghul Emperors of India and other Muslim patrons.[2] This is evidence also of the major influence in, and dominance of, the market for several centuries by Islamic rulers, patrons, and consumers in the lands of the Indian Ocean.

Entering the market at the end of the 19th century CE, the Maastricht ceramics also conformed, and in the same way, to this long-established factor. Maastricht thus followed in both the artistic and marketing patterns that had been established centuries earlier by other producers, principally their Chinese predecessors.

The result of all these influences and markets was that in the Indian Ocean the Maastricht and similar products, which had originally been meant as plates and bowls for modest homes in their home markets, became and were understood as a wholly different product, for wholly different classes, and for wholly different purposes. This change was reflected in responding designs and patterns.

These products now became a part of a different ceramic tradition—the tradition of Islamic ceramics, 'one of the most characteristic and singular of all the Islamic arts'.[3] This was reflected in the personal and state collections of Muslim rulers around the Indian Ocean.

1 Oliver Watson, *Ceramics From Islamic Lands: The Al-Sabah Collection, Kuwait National Museum* (New York, Thames & Hudson / Kuwait National Museum, 2005).

2 Ibid. 486 (for the Moghul Emperor Aurangzeb) and 490.

3 Ibid. Preface.

Though they appeared first on rural hearths, they ended up on banqueting tables in palaces. Though they were designs for peasants, they ended up being commissioned by kings. Though they were conceived for cheap use in the local countryside, they ended up valued on distant shores.

Consciously designed for a local low-income market, they unintendedly became symbols of prestige and social celebration for elite ruling classes in far-off lands.

And so in East Africa the result of all these influences was that the stolid Dutch Maastricht ceramics had become a wholly different product for a wholly different purpose. Manufactured in one tradition, they had become a part of a wholly different tradition. A global influence, the consumers had become the designers of a very different product.

The horse carriage and tea service from Queen Victoria were thus not the only signs of monarchy that Zanzibar and Hyderabad shared. They shared also the presence in their palaces of the Dutch- and English-produced Zanzibar plates, especially those with their attractive acknowledgement and display of Islamic symbols and calligraphy.

These Maastricht and similar plates may still be seen in the former palaces of the Nizam of Hyderabad in India and of the Sultan of Zanzibar, now preserved as museums, the palaces now also wan echoes of the empty *zidaka* mourned by Pate's great poet 200 years ago.

The uses on the East African coast (and in other parts around the Indian Ocean) of the Maastricht-type plates had significantly departed from the uses of the same product in Western Europe. Different social strata were using these products, and the plates and bowls were being put to different social uses. Plates and bowls were being put on mosque walls and on tombs. They were acquiring a decorative purpose absent in the countries of their manufacture.

All these historical and social factors mark out Zanzibar plates in Indian Ocean lands as an area of study distinct from the study of the same products in their native countries of manufacture—Holland, England, France, and Germany.

These plates are not of the precision of porcelain either in form or design. Instead they revel in the broad brush stroke, the uncaring bleed over outlines, the indelicate heaviness. Yet, in their ability to adapt, they found a cultural welcome and settled comfortably, as the consumers saw it, into the consumers' own very long tradition of usage of and ornamentation with such materials.

This essay thus offers a framework for the place of these late Dutch objects in the record and tradition of ceramics in the Islamic lands of the Indian Ocean, particularly the East African coast.

This part of our social and artistic history also emphasizes our regional context and the shared histories among Zanzibar-Pemba, Lamu, the Tanzania coast and mainland, and the Kenya coast and mainland, as well as among our neighbours around the Indian Ocean.

Sadiq Ghalia, who knew them best, has the final word: 'Zanzibar plates reflect not only aspects of Swahili architecture but also the habits of our people. These items were integral to our major religious and social celebrations. They were table finery brought out for special occasions like *Maulidi*, or circumcision ceremonies, or weddings. Zanzibar plates are an affectionate and inseparable part of Swahili culture and a part of our national heritage.'[4]

---

4 Personal interviews, 2007.

Base maps: Tanzania location map from Semhur; Africa map from Free Vector Maps.

Present-day
KENYA

Shee Umuro
Siu
Pate
Lamu
Manda
Kipini
Ungwana
Ngomeni
Mambrui
Gedi
Malindi
Kilifi
Mnarani
Takaungu
Jumba la Mtwana
Mombasa

N
W E
S

Present-day
TANZANIA

Pemba

Zanzibar
Bagamoyo
Kunduchi
Dar es Salaam

Mafia

Kilwa

Area
Enlarged

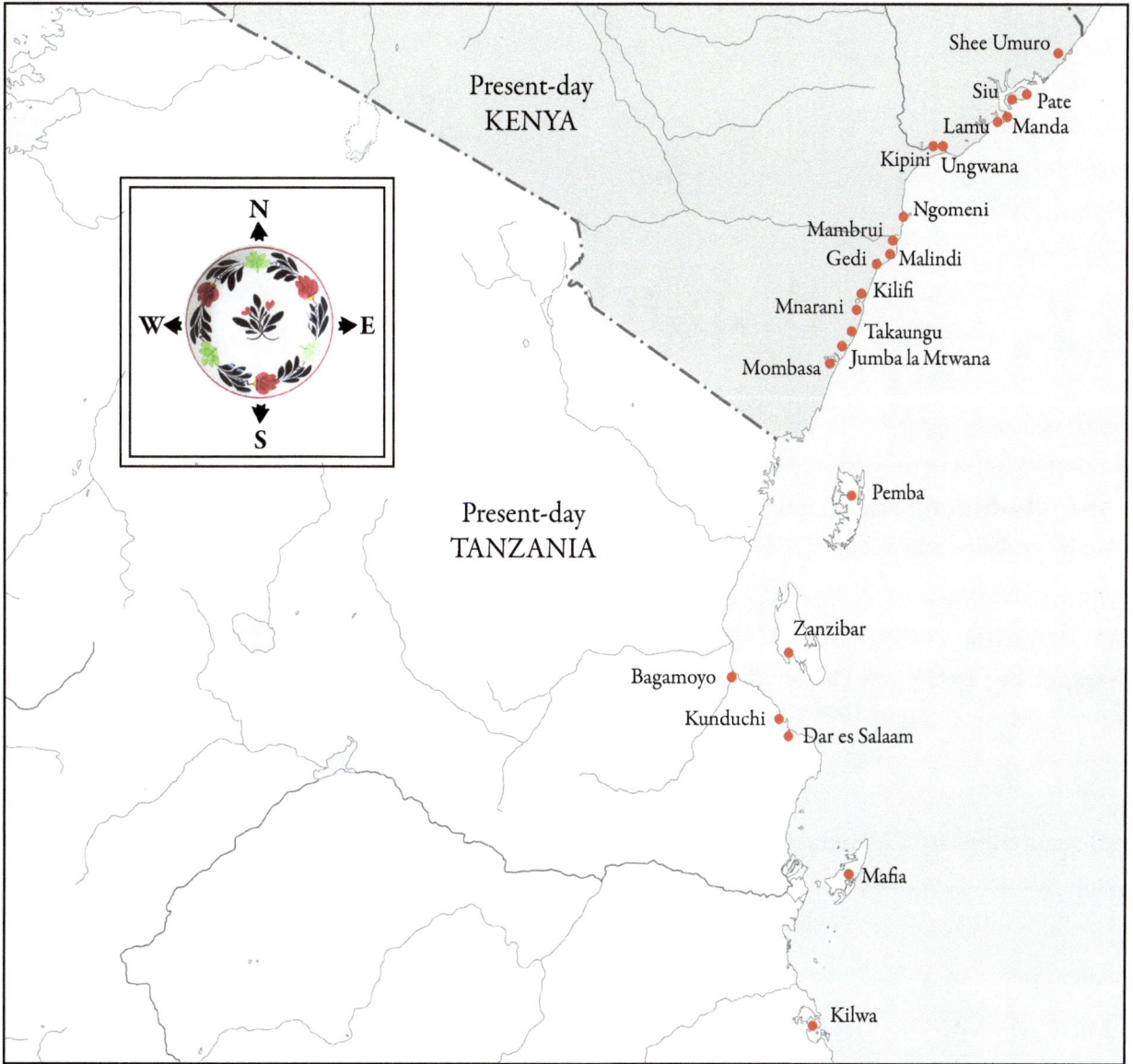

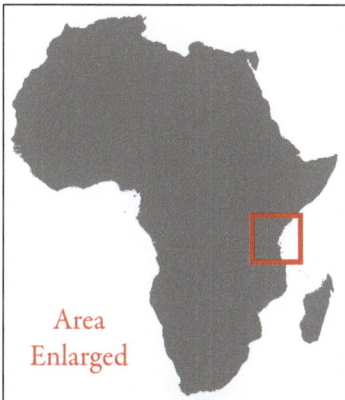

THE
EAST AFRICAN COAST

Sites mentioned in the text

BIBLIOGRAPHY

Abu, Khadija, 'The Significant Role of the Kanga Cloth in East Africa', BA thesis, Buckinghamshire Chilterns University College, 2001.

Abungu, George and **Lorna Abungu**, *Lamu: Kenya's Enchanted Island*, photographs by Carol Beckwith, Angela Fisher, David Coulson, and Nigel Pavitt; poetry by Ahamed Sheikh Nabhany; research by Linda Wiley Donley-Reid (New York, Rizzoli International Publications, 2009).

Aldrick, Judith, 'The Painted Plates of Zanzibar', *29 Kenya Past and Present* (1997), 26.

Aldrick, Judy, *The Sultan's Spymaster: Peera Dewji of Zanzibar* (Naivasha, Old Africa Books, 2015).

Alexander, John, 'The Archaeological Recognition of Religion: The Examples of Islam in Africa and "Urnfields" in Europe' in B. Burnham and J. Kingsbury (eds.), *Space, Hierarchy and Settlement* (Oxford, British Archaeological Reports, BAR S59, 215).

Allen, James de Vere, *Lamu* (Nairobi, Kenya Museum Society, 1972).

Allen, James de Vere, *Lamu Town: A Guide* (Lamu, Allen, 1977).

Allen, James de Vere (transl.) and **Sayyid Abdalla bin Ali bin Nasir**, *Al-Inkishafi: Catechism of a Soul* (Nairobi, East African Literature Bureau, 1977).

Beech, Mervyn, *Swahili Life* (Mombasa, Fort Jesus) n.d. [circa 1915].

Bogaers, Marie-Rose, *Drukdecors de Maastricht Aardewerk 1850–1900* (Lochem, Untiek Uitgenersmaatschappy Antiek Lochem bv).

Brown, Robert, *The Story of Africa and Its Explorers*, n.d. [circa 1892], n.p.

Chaudhuri, K. N., *Trade and Civilization in the Indian Ocean: An Economic History from the Rise of Islam to 1750* (Cambridge, Cambridge University Press, 1985).

Chittick, H. Neville, 'Unguja Ukuu: The Earliest Imported Pottery and One Abbasid Dinar', *Azania* I (1966), 161.

Chittick, H. Neville, 'Archaeological Finds from the Region of Lamu' in James de Vere Allen, *Lamu* (Nairobi, Kenya Museum Society, 1972), 29–31.

Chittick, Neville, 'Notes on Kilwa', *Tanganyika Notes and Records* No. 53 (October 1959), 179.

Chittick, Neville, 'East African Trade with the Orient' in D. S. Richards (ed.), *Islam and the Trade with Asia* (Oxford, Oxford University Press, 1970).

Chittick, Neville, 'Relics of the Past in the Region of Dar-es-Salaam, in Dar-es-Salaam City, Port and Region', *Tanganyika Notes and Records* No. 71 (1970), 65.

Chittick, Neville, *Kilwa: An Islamic Trading City on the East African Coast* (Nairobi, British Institute in Eastern Africa, 1974).

Crofton, R. H., *Zanzibar Affairs 1914–1933*, (London, Francis Edwards, 1953).

Datoo, Bashir A., *Port Development in East Africa* (Nairobi, East African Literature Bureau, 1975).

de Wit, Christel and **Zarina Patel,** 'Language of the Kanga', *Awaaz* Issue II (2004), 55, 56.

Donley-Reid, Linda Wiley, 'The Social Uses of Swahili Space and Objects', PhD thesis, Cambridge University, 1984.

Duyvendak, J. J. L., *China's Discovery of Africa* (London, 1949).

Fisher, S. W., *English Pottery and Porcelain Marks* (Slough, W. Foulsham, 1970).

Fitzpatrick, Mary, *Tanzania, Zanzibar and Pemba* (Lonely Planet Publications, August 1999), 174.

Freeman-Grenville, Dr. G. S. P., 'Chinese Porcelain in Tanganyika', *Tanganyika Notes and Records* No. 41 (1955), 63.

Freeman-Grenville, Dr. G. S. P., 'Some Problems of East African Coinage: From Early Times to 1890', *Tanganyika Notes and Records* No. 53 (October 1959), 250.

Garlake, P., *The Early Islamic Architecture of the East African Coast* (London, 1966).

Ghaidan, Usam, 'Swahili Art of Lamu', *African Art* (Autumn 1971).

Ghaidan, Usam, *Lamu: A Study of the Swahili Town* (Nairobi, East African Literature Bureau, 1975).

Ghaidan, Usam, *Lamu: A Study in Conservation* (Nairobi, East African Literature Bureau, 1976).

Gouveia, Alexandria, 'A Cultured Pearl', *Oryx* (November 2008), 64–70.

Grube, Ernest J., *The World of Islam* (London, Paul Hamlyn, 1966).

Hanby, Jeanette and **David Bygott,** *Kanga: 101 Uses* (1984; 2nd edition, Nairobi, Haria's Stamps, 2008).

Hill, M. F., *Permanent Way* Vol. I (Nairobi, East African Railways and Harbours, 1950).

Hourani, George, *Arab Seafaring in the Indian Ocean in Ancient and Mediaeval Times* (Princeton, Princeton University Press, 1951; 1995 edition).

Ingrams, W. H., *Zanzibar: Its History and Its People* (London, H. F. & G. Witherby, 1931).

Insoll, Timothy, 'Archaeology and the Reconstruction of Religious Identity in Africa (and Beyond)', *Azania* XXXIX (2004), 195, 197–200.

Issa, Amina Ameir, 'The Burial of the Elite in Nineteenth Century Zanzibar Stone Town' in Abdul Sheriff (ed.), *The History and Conservation of Zanzibar Stone Town* (Zanzibar, Department of Archives, Museums and Antiquities / London, James Currey, 1995), 67–80.

Jaffer, Amin, *Furniture from British India and Ceylon* (London, Victoria & Albert Publications, 2001).

Jafferji, Javed and **Elie Losleben,** *Swahili Style* (Zanzibar, Gallery Publications, 2005).

Jafferji, Javed and **Nadin Hadi,** *Kanga Wisdom: A Collection of Kanga Sayings* (Zanzibar, Gallery Publications, 2007).

Khan, Kalandar Kamal, *The Swahili Architecture of Lamu, Kenya: Oral Tradition and Space* (Saarbruken, Lambert Academic Publishing, 2010).

Kiriama, Herman O., *The Swahili of the Kenya Coast* (Mombasa, Eight Publishers / National Museums of Kenya, 2005).

Kirkman, James, *Gedi National Park: Plan and Explanatory Notes* (Nairobi, Kenya National Parks Trustees, Government Printer, March 1949).

Kirkman, James, 'Excavations at Ras Mkumbu on the Island of Pemba', *Tanganyika Notes and Records* No. 53 (October 1959), 161.

Kirkman, James, 'Fort Jesus Museum Collection', *Kenya Past and Present* Vol. 1 No. 2 (April 1972), 4.

Kirkman, James, *Fort Jesus* (Oxford, The Clarendon Press, 1974).

Kirkman, James, *Gedi* (Nairobi, National Museums of Kenya, 1975, 8th edition).

Knappert, Jan, *Four Centuries of Swahili Verse: A Literary History and Anthology* (London, Heinemann Educational, 1979).

Kusimba, Chapurukha Makokha, *The Rise and Fall of Swahili States* (Walnut Creek, CA, AltaMira/ Sage, 1999).

Kusimba, Makokha, 'Chinese Ceramics in the Fort Jesus Museum Collection', *26 Kenya Past and Present* 55 (1994).

Martin, Esmond Bradley, *Malindi Vergangenheit Und Gegenwart* (Nairobi, Kenya Museum Society, 1972) [including photographs (from 1935) of pillar tombs].

Martin, Esmond Bradley, *Zanzibar: Tradition and Revolution* (London, Hamish Hamilton, 1978).

Mathew, G., *The Culture of the East African Coast in the Seventeenth and Eighteenth Centuries* (1956).

Mazrui, Alamin M. and **Ibrahim Noor Shariff,** *The Swahili: Idiom and Identity of an African People* (Trenton, Africa World Press, 1994).

Menzies, Gavin, *1421: The Year China Discovered the World* (London, Bantam Press, 2002).

Middleton, John, *The World of the Swahili: An African Mercantile Civilization* (New Haven, Yale University Press, 1992).

Moon, Karen, *Kilwa Kisiwani: Ancient Port City of the East African Coast* (Dar es Salaam, Government of Tanzania, 2005).

Nicholls, C. S., *The Swahili Coast: Politics, Diplomacy and Trade on the East African Littoral 1798–1856* (London, Allen & Unwin, 1971).

Pannikar, K. M., *Asia and Western Dominance* (New Delhi, Asia Publishing, 1953).

Pannikar, K. M., *Geographical Factors in Indian History* (Bombay, Bharatiya Vidya Bhavan, 1959).

Pearce, Major Francis Barrow, *Zanzibar: The Island Metropolis of Eastern Africa* (London, Unwin, 1920).

Penrad, Jean-Claude, 'The Social Fallout of Individual Death: Graves and Cemeteries in Zanzibar' in Abdul Sheriff (ed.), *The History and Conservation of Zanzibar Stone Town* (Zanzibar, Department of Archives, Museums and Antiquities / London, James Currey, 1995), 82.

Playne, S. and **F. Gayle,** *East Africa (British)* (London, Foreign and Colonial Compiling and Publishing Company, 1909).

Polling, A., 'Boerenbont aardewerk uit de fabriek van Petrus Regout', *Antiek* (1988), 23, 267.

Polling, A., *Maastrichts Ceramiek: Merken en Dateringen* (Lochem, Untiek Uitgenersmaatschappy Antiek Lochem bv, 2001).

Revington, T. M., 'Note on the Bowl Mentioned on Page 36 of Tanganyika Notes and Records No. 1 of March 1936', *Tanganyika Notes and Records* No. 2 (October 1936), 110.

Rice, David Talbot, *Islamic Art* (London, Thames & Hudson, 1965, 1975).

Rickens-Koerner, Antje, *Stone Town Styles of East Coast Africa* (Cape Town, Bell Roberts, 2003).

Robinson, A. E., 'Notes on Saucer and Bowl Decorations on Houses, Mosques and Temples', *Tanganyika Notes and Records* No. 10 (December 1940).

Romero, Patricia W., *Lamu: History, Society and Family in an East African Port City* (Princeton, Marcus Wiener, 1997).

Ruete, Emily (born Salme, Princess of Oman and Zanzibar), *Memoirs of an Arabian Princess from Zanzibar* (1886, Zanzibar, The Gallery, 1998 revised translation).

Sassoon, Caroline, *Blue and White Animals* (Mombasa, Museum Trustees of Kenya / Kenya Museum Society, 1974).

Sassoon, Caroline, *Chinese Porcelain in Fort Jesus* (Mombasa, National Museums of Kenya, 1975).

Sassoon, Caroline, *Chinese Porcelain Marks from Coastal Sites in Kenya: Aspects of Trade in the Indian Ocean XIV–XIX Centuries* (1978), BAR International Series (Supplementary), 43, 3.

Sassoon, Hamo, *Kunduchi: A Guide to the Ruins at Kunduchi* (Dar es Salaam, Ministry of Community Development and National Culture, 1966).

Sassoon, Hamo, 'The Coastal Town of Jumba La Mtwana', *12 Kenya Past and Present* 2 (1980).

Sassoon, Hamo, *Jumba La Mtwana Guide* (Nairobi, Kenya Museum Society / Friends of Fort Jesus, 1981).

Sayyid Abdalla bin Ali bin Nasir and **James de Vere Allen** (transl.), *Al-Inkishafi: Catechism of a Soul* (Nairobi, East African Literature Bureau, 1977).

Schoppert, Peter, Tara Sosrowardoyo, and **Soedarmadji Damais,** *Java Style* (London, Thames & Hudson, 1997).

Selaued, Eivind Heldass (ed.), *The Indian Ocean in the Ancient Period: Definite Places, Trans-Local Exchange* (Oxford, Archaeopress, British Archive Reports, 2007).

Sheriff, Abdul, *Slaves, Spices and Ivory in Zanzibar* (London, James Currey, 1987).

Sheriff, Abdul and **Ed Ferguson** (eds.), *Zanzibar Under Colonial Rule* (London, James Currey, 1991).

Sheriff, Abdul (ed.), *The History and Conservation of Zanzibar Stone Town* (Zanzibar, Department of Archives, Museums and Antiquities / London, James Currey, 1995).

Shuyi, Kan, *Inspired By Japan and China: The Egawa Collection of European Ceramics* (Singapore, Asian Civilizations Museum, 2011).

Stiles, Daniel, 'The Ports of East Africa, the Comoros and Madagascar: Their Place in the Indian Ocean Trade AD 1–1500', *24 Kenya Past and Present* 27 (1992).

Sutton, John E. G., *The East African Coast: An Historical and Archaeological Review* (Dar es Salaam, Historical Association of Tanzania / East African Publishing House, 1966).

Sutton, John E. G., *Kilwa: A History of the Ancient Swahili Town with a Guide to the Monuments of Kilwa Kisiwani and Adjacent Islands* (Nairobi, British Institute in Eastern Africa, 2000).

Tanner, R. E. S., 'Some Chinese Pottery Found at Kilwa Kisiwani', *Tanganyika Notes and Records* No. 32 (January 1952).

The Economist, 'China Beat Columbus To It, Perhaps' (14 January 2006), 80.

Trimingham, J. S., *Islam in East Africa* (London, 1966).

Troughear, Tony, 'Khangas, Bangles and Baskets', *16 Kenya Past and Present* (1983), 11.

Vanco, John and **Kelly Armour,** *Kanga: Wrap Garments from East Africa* (Erie, PA, Erie Art Museum, 2008).

Volker, T., *Porcelain and the Dutch East India Company* (Leiden, 1971).

Watson, Oliver, *Ceramics from Islamic Lands: The Al-Sabah Collection, Kuwait National Museum* (New York, Thames & Hudson / Kuwait National Museum, 2005).

Wilding, Richard, *The Far Eastern Pottery Collection of the National Museum at Dar-es-Salaam* (Nairobi, British Institute of History and Archaeology of Eastern Africa, 1971).

Wilding, Richard, 'The Ceramics of the Lamu Archipelago', PhD thesis, University of Nairobi, 1977.

Wilding, Richard, 'Panels, Pillars and Posterity: Ancient Tombs on the North Kenyan Coast, A Preliminary Study' (Mombasa, *Fort Jesus Occasional Papers* No. 6, 1988).

Wilkinson, Charles K., *Nishapur: Pottery of the Early Islamic Period* (New York, Metropolitan Museum of Art, n.d.).

Wilkinson, Charles K., *Iranian Ceramics* (New York, Asia House Gallery Publications, 1963).

Woody, Howard, 'International Postcards (Their History, Production and Distribution c. 1895 to 1915)' in Christraud M. Geary and Virginia-Lee Webb (eds.), *Delivering Views: Distant Cultures in Early Postcards* (Washington, Smithsonian, 1998).

Ylvisaker, Marguerite, *Lamu in the Nineteenth Century: Land, Trade and Politics* (Boston, African Studies Center, Boston University, 1979).

Acknowledgements and thanks are gratefully offered to:

Sadiq Ghalia, for sharing the treasures of his incomparable collection and his knowledge with us and others with so much generosity, enthusiasm, and delight

Teresa and Chris Orme-Smith, who welcomed us so warmly into their long study of the subject

Prof. Abdul Sheriff, who carefully went through the early text and, applying his great erudition of the region, sent meticulous notes that enabled the authors to make significantly improved revisions

Dr. Kalandar Khan, who enriched the text with his learning and love of the coast, its architecture, and its literature

And to:

The Librarians at the British Institute for East Africa/IFRA, Nairobi

The Librarian at the Fort Jesus Library, Mombasa

The Librarians at the National Museums of Kenya, Nairobi

The Librarian at the Court of Appeal of Kenya, Nairobi

The Kenya Museum Society, Nairobi

Sheroo and Noshir Billimoria, Mumbai

Salim Ghalia

Nicky Orme-Smith

Sia Nowrojee

Gabriel Abraham

Elchi Nowrojee

Farouk Issa of Philips, Mumbai

And to:

Edward Miller, for a beautiful book

The text has had the grateful benefit of the study of several collections, but particularly the Sadiq Ghalia Collection, the Orme-Smith Collection, the Elchi Nowrojee Collection of Postcards, the Villoo Nowrojee Collection, and the collections of the Beit-el-Ajaib and Palace Museums in Zanzibar, the National Museum of Tanzania in Dar es Salaam, Fort Jesus Museum in Mombasa, the Lamu Museum, the Gedi Museum, and the Malindi Museum.

9789966736031